INTEGRITY IS EVERYTHING

JOHN LAVENIA

Integrity is Everything
Published by Lavenia Enterprises, LLC

ISBN: 1-4392-1596-0
ISBN-13: 9781439215968

First edition.

Printed in the United States of America

Cover design by Working Bee Studio

This book is available in special quantity discounts when purchased in bulk. For information, please contact Lavenia Enterprises, 4470 W Sunset Blvd. #320, Los Angeles, California 90027, USA or on the World Wide Web at www.johnlavenia.com.

INTEGRITY

-Adherence to moral and ethical principles;
soundness of moral character; honesty.

-A sound, unimpaired, or perfect condition, completeness.

-The quality or condition of being whole,
undivided or undiminished.

Contents

ACKNOWLEDGEMENTS

I'd like to thank all those who have actively taken part in the development of human potential on this planet. Through this book I have endeavored to remind people of the insights you have offered to the human race throughout time, as they occur now in my life. It is my honor to carry this torch which so many have borne. To name all the visionaries who have touched me would require another book, and the knowledge that more are constantly arriving gives me strength.

I'd also like to express my heartfelt appreciation to the friends I have met on the path. Their roles have been many and their backgrounds diverse. My parents - Joseph Lavenia and Diana-Marie Maione. It was my mother who maintained hope at times in my life when none seemed possible; and my father who introduced me to new ways of thinking (and not-thinking) which serve me still. My grandparents, who suspended judgment and offered solace to a troubled youth. Dr. Alan Cavaiola, Kip Campbell and George Lavenia, who told me like it is.

To Gene and Heather Braxton, thank you for being people who take hold of the reigns and show the world what's possible when people act with integrity. Thank you also for your enthusiastic input as I completed this book.

To Shane and Michelle Krider, greater friends could not be asked for. You arrived in my life at a time of opportunity and showed me how to play at a whole new level. Shane, you are a true master, appearing as a common man. At times you said little, but conveyed much. The tree of plenty continues to bear fruit; the only condition is that I ask.

And to my wife, Shannon, what words could express the love and gratitude I feel for having you in my life. You are a radiating example of power and beauty to all who meet you. You are an embodiment of graciousness, and an inspiration to many. You took principles in this book and accomplished in one year what took me ten. Thank you for being my partner in this journey of life, for your belief in me, and for your belief in yourself.

This is typically where authors thank their editor; but since I edited this entire book myself, a task which I will never do again, I'll have to save that for next time. So let me end here by thanking you for reading it. It is with great respect that I offer you this work. May you find yourself in action after reading it.

Integrity Is Everything

Meet The Guru

This book is for people who value results above platitudes and theories. What you're about to read is a full-disclosure explanation of a discovery which has brought me from a miserable existence of quiet desperation and mediocrity, to a recognized leader in business, a successful partner in my marriage, a person in perfect health... a person whose life works.

Let me confess right now — had you known me twenty years ago, you probably would have never imagined that I was someone who would become wildly successful, or write a book disseminating the principles I have used to do so. Struggle and unhappiness were constants in my life at one time, and I wasn't discreet about it. Sure, I wanted success as we all do, but it seemed so elusive and foreign. Like many people, I started seeking answers to the questions of life. How did successful people get that way? Why do most people fail? Why do I seem to work so hard for such meager results?

I started studying some of the greatest thinking in history — the Bible, the Bhagavad-Gita, Buddhist and Zen teachings, Lao Tzu, Ben Franklin, Napoleon Hill, Goethe, Jefferson, Hubbard, Emerson, Muktananda, Yogananda, etc. I started to see some gains in my life, but despite all available knowledge, I still hadn't broken through to the results I really wanted. I would go to seminars, read the books, buy the courses, etc. — I had a head full of knowledge but I still wasn't getting the results. And I noticed other people weren't either! It doesn't take a terribly perceptive person to observe that most people just aren't living the life they truly want. In fact, some of the people who have the most to say about their beliefs demonstrate the least *applied* belief in what they are supposedly in alignment with.

And then something "clicked" for me. Something happened that caused my great intentions to start bearing fruit in my life. And the results were abundant. Sometimes I was shocked at the difference between my newfound success and the struggling I had previously done. I experienced complete turnarounds in my life – and it actually became simple (even fun) to succeed. I saw results show up in my life as a result of applying some simple principles. I then applied those same principles to other areas of my life, and got results there as well. It's as if one switch after another turned on, and my experience of that part of my life had completely changed. After a while, success became predictable - even common – as common as the struggle or "falling short" that most people experience in their lives every day. Was I lucky?

I realized that something is happening for me that is not happening for the majority of people. What could it be? So, after much urging from friends and business associates who know my work, I've decided to write this book to distill down after 20 years of study what has actually worked in my life. None of the principles I will speak of are new. I don't have any new truth for you. The point is that I've acted on these things, and it's produced success, it's produced wealth, it's produced results that are pretty uncommon.

Now I think it would be helpful if I shared with you a bit about my background. Not that the past dictates where one is going, but it may give some context as to why this book may seem bold. I didn't write this so people could stay comfortable, or curl up with a good book and be cozy by the fireplace. It may also serve as a testament that the principles I will present in this book *do* work, and to the tremendous magnitude that they work.

I was born in New Jersey and spent nearly all of my young life there. When I was four years old my parents were divorced. I lived with my mother, who remarried two years later. As it turns out, the man she chose as her second husband was an ex-military man and worked a menial job. He lacked stability. Until the age of 13 I lived in poverty and abuse, and at times would hide under my bed in fear, or shut myself in a closet to try and escape the helplessness I constantly felt. I had virtually no interaction with other children. I was a social outcast. I developed a nervous condition, according to doctors, and was given medicine and psychiatry. When that didn't work, it was determined that I needed more discipline. I was always being punished for something. The constant emotional turbulence I experienced caused me to be sick with a cold, flu or tonsillitis about every two weeks.

I was not able to develop a relationship with my natural father, and was taught that to do so would be disloyal to the family. (He was, and is, a successful businessman.) In times when he was given an opportunity to visit me and my brother, I was warned that he was an enemy, and that I dared not speak of anything that occurred in my daily life. It would be difficult to describe the emotional state of a child when his life, his health and even his thoughts are an issue of perpetual conflict between his parents. It wasn't until later in life that I developed a relationship with my father, and discovered a person who was completely different than what I had been told.

At age 13, after years of living in fear, suppression and violence, I was relieved when my mother divorced her second husband. I felt a sudden freedom which I immediately used to overcompensate for my previous years. I was an emotionally explosive adolescent with a head full of hate and no purpose. I started running the streets with drunks and drug addicts, and before long I fit right in. Escaping reality to the best of my ability through mind altering chemicals was how I dealt with the next three years of my life. But my self-hatred worsened. By age 15 I could be diagnosed with any number of depression-related labels by the psychiatric community.

Fortunately for me, at the still young age of 16, I was introduced to various personal development principles and for the first time I had hope. I learned that I wasn't unique in my suffering, and that something could be done about it. This is when my life started to change.

I somehow finished high school, decided to take up a trade and went to school to learn how to be a diesel mechanic. I was able to work with my brain and my hands and get a positive result. This was very gratifying. After some years in the mechanical fields, I realized I could run the company I was working for better than my boss. So I resigned from my job and went into business for myself. I bought a franchise purely on borrowed funds in a related field (tools) and was now an entrepreneur. All the while I had been expanding my knowledge of human potential and how the mind works.

Life was grand, except for the 90 hour work weeks and the accounts-receivable and the inventory and the shipping and receiving, etc. After a few years I resigned from that business and experimented with others. I still hadn't made my mark. I was still struggling financially. It was around this time that I met my wife, Shannon, through a personal ad on the internet. (How else does a sober guy in his twenties who works all the time meet people?) The chips were down for me financially and I wound up selling cars for the next four years.

After five years together, Shannon and I married, which I didn't think would ever happen in my life because of the misery I witnessed growing up. But it appears that the past does not necessarily equal the future. The next big development in my life was about to happen, in the area of money and career, and before long I had made millions. (You can learn more about the details of that at www.JohnLavenia.com) Through the use of principles that I'll speak about in this book I became a recognized leader in the direct-selling industry and I began teaching others how they too could have the success they want. And the good news is, it doesn't have to take 20 years of study.

Now let me say this: As great as it is to witness success in my own life, it has been even more profound to see it duplicated in the lives of others. Having observed how most people continue to struggle in life, I started to wonder if I was somehow unique or special because I had made such tremendous gains. But the principles I applied were so simple. Would they work for other people too? In every case, the answer was yes. 100% of the time, when people adopted, internalized and acted on the ideas I shared with them they succeeded in getting what they were after. And the results seemed almost superhuman. I've seen failing marriages become stronger than ever. I've watched people transform their bodies from obesity and sickliness to health and vitality. I witnessed a single mother who went from poverty and desperation to self-made millionaire in just two years. I watched a corporate burnout regain purpose in his life and completely transform his relationship with his children, not to mention quadruple his income.

When people get results like these, others marvel at their accomplishments. Successful people have always been the minority, and with that success comes a certain degree of recognition. But understand that these people have simply applied principles that will work for *anyone* who cares enough about their own results to use them. I'd like to tell you that they are the "secrets of success", because I know that sells, but they aren't secrets. In fact, countless people have been exposed to the same ideas I have. Most people know what to do; they're just not doing it.

Unlike the average person who, at best, takes a part-time approach to improving their life, successful people discern and internalize empowering principles and integrate them with their behavior. Having consulted with thousands of people throughout the world, I have found that people who have chosen to actually *live* the ideas that we'll discuss have had results that the masses would sooner disbelieve than accept as a real possibility. But, of course, they are not the masses. They have developed an *experiential knowledge* of true success principles, and *they developed it for themselves.* The answers to success which we all seek will be found in ourselves as we observe, consider and act. It is my intention to explain, unequivocally, my understanding of what has actually worked in my life. You will no-doubt gain distinctions from my experiences. But know that you will make these distinctions for yourself, because the only truth that matters is the truth that's alive in you. I don't benefit from your interpretation of some great teaching, even if the teaching came from a great master. The truth has to be alive in me for me to benefit from it. If *you* take just a couple of distinctions from this book and it allows principles to start showing up in *your* life, in your daily activities, in your behavior, then your results must, *absolutely must*, reflect increase.

Do not believe in anything simply because you have heard it.
Do not believe in anything simply because it is spoken and rumored by many.
Do not believe in anything simply because it is found written in your religious books.
Do not believe in anything merely on the authority of your teachers and elders.

Do not believe in traditions because they have been handed down for many generations.

But after observation and analysis, when you find that anything agrees with reason and is conducive to the good and benefit of one and all, then accept it and live up to it.

Gautama Buddha (563-483 BC)

So this book is about the actual application of principles. Principles that I've identified and that *I have acted upon,* and because of that action, because of my *integrity* to these principles, they showed up in my life as results.

You see, my approach to getting results in my life - my approach to self mastery - is a full-time approach. It's a full-time reality in my life. I don't teach anything that I have not personally experienced and benefitted from, and I have no interest in pretending to be an expert in areas that I'm not. That's the difference between what I want to give you and the majority of the "self-help" crap that keeps people running in circles. I don't have any magical pixie-dust or "new age" (whatever that is) doctrine. I don't have any new truth for you. I'm not your guru. And I certainly don't think you need another modern-day messiah to sell you the next "secret missing ingredient" so you can finally get on with your life. So let me come right out and say that I am no one's guru. Except my own, I guess, if you really get down to it.

That reminds me of a story. And I think it's an appropriate story for the beginning part of this book, because it reveals an approach that you could take to keep this whole idea of self-mastery - this idea of making big strides in your life - very simple. And really, it kind of frames the whole book and the kind of ideas that I think are in play for people who "get it" sooner rather than later.

This guy (I don't know the guy's name, but it's this guy) is having a challenge in his life. He has a problem with his relationships. And so, he is seeking answers in his life. And he hears of a great guru who lives in the wilderness on top of a nearby mountain. So he decides to go see the guru on top of the mountain. He begins his quest and ultimately meets the guru and tells of his troubles. At the end of the meeting the guru says, "My child, you are free to go, you will no longer have that problem. You are healed. Live long and prosper."

So the guy goes back to his life, and sure enough, that problem is no longer happening in his life. Later he has a different problem that shows up (perhaps it's one of money or parenting or whatever) so he goes again to the guru, because this was very effective the first time. And he goes to meet the guru and tells him (or her) about his problem, and the guru assures him that this problem is also handled now, and he can go have a great life. And sure enough, results! Spectacular!

This routine happens a couple more times. And one day, the guy is thinking, "You know, I have a problem, and I go to the guru, and he tells me the problem is gone, and it is gone. And yet, what's happening here? The guru didn't cast a spell. He didn't play with crystals or relics. He didn't even burn incense. He didn't *do* a damn thing! And I believed him! And I go home and, guess what, the problem's gone!"

Suddenly, the words "Your faith has healed you" ring in his mind.

And then the question, "So who's the guru?"

And the guy gets it, that *he's* the guru. By going through some external source, by hearing the words of *an other*, he got to have some faith. Faith in himself. Faith in the workings of the universe. Faith in the perfection that already exists, and he is healed by his belief.

So, big surprise, now you know who the guru is. Say hi to yourself. As you read this book I'd like for you to stop looking outside of yourself for your answer. Your answer is already within. But your answer is *revealed by you, through your action*. Keep this in mind as you go. And please consider that from this point forward your life could take a whole new direction, if that's what you truly want. You are so capable. I don't believe you are; I know you are. By the end of this book, you will know it too (if you don't already).

And one other note before we move on: Do yourself a favor and don't go past any words you don't fully understand as you read. As you can probably tell, my writing is very conversational and my intention is that you understand it. At no point did I intend to write a highbrow, esoteric thesis aimed at post-graduate psychology students. But if you should find a word that you are not comfortable having a conversation with yourself, grab a dictionary and get the meaning of it fully. I recommend you do this whenever you read anything. I do this myself, especially when I'm reading older books. I found the English in use in older writings to be much more advanced than it is today.

That being said, understanding what the author is saying makes whatever I'm reading exponentially more useable; and it's great to be able to use what I learn. And I suspect that's why you're reading this book in the first place.

THE DIFFERENCE

I had a dream. I was walking through some sort of open-air bazaar – like the ones where tourists go to haggle over wood carvings, seashell necklaces, coconut art, pottery and other trinkets from whatever location they are visiting. Something was different about this one though. There were no stray animals running around in the street, nobody offered to buy the shoes off my feet and everyone spoke the same language. I started to have a look around at the various merchant's wares, and noticed that there were none of the typical arts and crafts being sold. Instead, it appeared that the only thing for sale was some sort of plaque – just planks of wood of various shapes and sizes. I thought this was interesting.

Suddenly, there was an outburst. A crowd of people had gathered around some of the vendors in the distance and were making quite a commotion. I rushed up to see what was going on. It appeared that the local craftsmen had just completed a fresh batch of product, and a buying frenzy had commenced. I got up on my toes to see as best I could through the crowd. One merchant held up a plaque with a single word printed on it: Failure. The crowd went crazy over it. It was painted in blue and had sparkly gold glitter around the word and the edges. There was no haggling. Instead, it was a bidding war. I heard someone yell, "Five thousand!" Then another shouted, "Ten thousand!" Then everybody started yelling and utter chaos broke out. Finally the piece was sold for several million dollars. It was amazing.

Then another vendor held up a plaque with the word: Misery. This one was red and yellow with rainbow colored glitter. Again, the people went nuts. Other plaques had words like Struggle, Conflict, Suffering, Disease and Pathetic. All were done up in glittery splendor. But as spectacular as the product was, even more awe-inspiring were the prices. People were spending everything they had on these things, and they were arguing amongst each other while doing it. Fights broke out and everything. People started hitting each other with their plaques. It was all very confusing to me.

I couldn't take any more of this crowd, so I backed off and started to move away. I don't think one person even noticed I was there. They were all so preoccupied, it's like I was invisible. I started to wander down the street to a less crowded area. I saw two men standing near a table and speaking casually with each other. One man was a merchant and the other was a friend or a customer. As I got closer, the merchant greeted me. The other tipped his hat. I said, "Hello." Behind the table the merchant had a pile of wooden planks of various shapes and sizes. None of them had anything written on them.

As if reading my mind, the merchant said, "Crazy, isn't it?" as he glanced down the street toward the crowd. I agreed, and was relieved to have found a couple of sane people who I could communicate with.

I asked him, "What are those people thinking?"

He answered, "They're not."

His friend gave a slight chuckle.

Then the merchant asked me, "Would you like a plaque?"

I said, "What do you got?"

"Whatever you want." he said.

I said, "Great, I'll take one that says Success."

The merchant selected a piece of wood out of the pile. He put it down on the table and pulled a black magic marker out of his pocket. He handed me the marker and said, "Is black okay?"

I said, "Sure." I took the marker and created my masterpiece in about 12 seconds.

"Beautiful" said the merchant.

"What do I owe you?" I asked.

"Two dollars. And that includes the hardware to hang it on a wall or stand it on a table. Here you go."

I gave him a $5 bill and said, "Here's two dollars for the wood, and three for the conversation. You guys have a great day."

"You do the same." The merchant replied. His friend tipped his hat, and I walked off into the sunset. The End.

I've got some great news for you if you're someone who is serious about experiencing the good things that life has to offer. For one, you are already in possession of the most vital elements of success, whether you know it or not. Secondly, the price of success is not greater than the price of failure. And what's more, there are no long lines or angry mobs to deal with at the success-merchant's table.

Think about this for a moment. When you put this book down you are going to think some thoughts. I have no idea what those thoughts are going to be, but those thoughts will cause some feelings to come up in you. Those feelings will lead to you taking some sort of action. Those actions will render a result.

Now, if the thoughts you think are those which fit comfortably with your current self-image, your current idea of who you are, then your emotions, actions and results will pretty much be like they are now. For some people, life is a journey of great victory and triumph, full of possibilities, success and abundance. For others it is a life of mediocrity and defeat. Wouldn't it be great if we could choose?

We can... In fact, we do.

Both the successful person and the failure get results in their life. Both have the same resources in terms of time, physical matter, thought, and the ability to act. And yet, their results may be light-years apart. One may have health while the other experiences illness. One may have beautiful relationships while the other lives in discord. One may earn more money in a month than the other earns in a lifetime.

Both individuals experience cycles of thought, feeling, action and result. This works perfectly, every time. So if we really think about it, we will realize that there is no such thing as "failure" in this scenario. There will always be a result which shows up in direct correlation with the thoughts, feelings and actions of the individual. Therefore, *the same energy* that people put into taking actions which guarantee failure *would guarantee success* if they chose different actions.

So what we are addressing in this book is the *cause* of a person's behavior - the thoughts which form the character of the individual. While it is easy to look at effects and philosophize about them, or attempt to put a band-aid on them, it is much more effective to treat causes and enjoy natural, lasting results. There is an easily observable difference in the circumstances and results of people, based on their willingness or unwillingness to address the cause of the results in their life. The observation of this difference is sometimes startling, if we're willing to look, as the folly of the masses is often nothing less than insane, or at least downright stupid.

There is no sin except stupidity.
Oscar Wilde (1854 – 1900)

Picture this example: You're in a grocery store. You are in line at the checkout counter and in front of you is a person who is at least 50 pounds overweight. They're yelling at their kids, who are totally unruly and pulling candy off the candy rack, which is positioned on the right and extends down almost to the floor. In their shopping cart you see the most sugar-laden, high-carb, high-fat, low-nutrition selections possible. And their cart is filled with it. Not a vegetable in sight, but lots of soda pop, TV-dinners and cheese-spread that squirts out of a can. Once they manage to put the final package of "food" on the counter, they reach over to the gossip-rag display (magazine rack) on the left which is conveniently positioned for those last-minute impulse buyers. They take a magazine off the rack which has an air-brushed photo of some celebrity on the cover and a headline that reads, "Get Slim Instantly! New Hollywood diet makes losing weight easy! Effortlessly shed those extra pounds with the secrets of the stars!"

Have you ever seen this? I have, countless times. After all, if being healthy and alert was as simple as proper nutrition and exercise, wouldn't everyone do it? Maybe they're just not lucky? Maybe they need another diet pill? Or perhaps a different drug to help them with their nerves – the one the TV advertisement told them to ask their doctor about. Or maybe they can put their kids on Ritalin?

The reality of the situation is that this person's outer circumstances are a direct reflection of something taking place inside them. And this didn't happen overnight. This is a habitual cycle of thought, feeling, action and result in full swing. There is no doubt that they feel like a victim, and they can't figure out why they struggle to lose weight or be effective as a parent. Can we sympathize with them? We can. But should we? Would our sympathy serve anyone? Would it empower them to take new action or go in a new direction? Our sympathy serves no one – not them, and not you either.

It takes a lot of energy to fail; the same energy that it takes to succeed. I'm not here to tell you that success is easy – it isn't. But neither is failure. Both come with a price. So it's a good idea to develop some self-determinism about which one we are going to experience. When people recognize that they are powerful in their ability to choose, powerful in their use of thought, and that they are able to take whatever actions are necessary for the fulfillment of their goals it is a very liberating thing. But many people don't really believe they are powerful, and that they are co-creators of their destiny. I have a very close friend named Shane Krider who hosts seminars and training events for his company, and I heard him once say on a teleconference, "Most people are like giants drowning in three feet of water!"

If people don't believe they are powerful, then they get to *not* be powerful in their life, and they will very *successfully* demonstrate weakness and ineffectiveness in their life. The fact is still the fact - that it is *their* energy they are putting into getting their results. And if we open our eyes and take an objective view, we can identify how people participate in causing the situations in their life that they find unpleasant. The more we pull ourselves out of self-imposed blindness, the more glaringly obvious this becomes to us, not just in the lives of other people, but in our own lives as well. We see that we are actually demonstrating results in our lives, year in and year out, which are perfectly congruent with our innermost beliefs about ourselves and our possibilities.

Why then would a seemingly rational person continue to engage in decisions that do not bring them success, all the while justifying how those decisions are right and how they are "doing their best"? It's as if something keeps tripping them up. To answer this, let's take a look at another example from the health and fitness realm. Being an avid weight-lifter, I find it easy to draw examples from sports and other physical disciplines. See if you can find a common thread in the two scenarios.

Recently while I was at the gym doing my workout I noticed something very interesting. I go to a large fitness center, and there can be 50 people or more there at any given time. On this particular day my iPod battery died, and as punishment I had to listen to the R&B love songs that were playing on the overhead sound system. While using one of the machines, I had a view of a large portion of the main room. I looked around and saw that most of the people there were completely out of shape! (I'm being generous with my description.)

Sure, there were the heavily-muscled types working out like madmen. I saw them too. And there were the girls with the extra-tight, color-coordinated workout suits that have "Pink" or some other meaningless word embroidered across their ass while they use the "leg-split-bend-over-and-stretch-your-thighs" machine. *Everyone* saw them. But about 80% of the people there had terrible results. And they didn't all just show up there as newbies. I've been going to that gym for years, and so have a lot of the people there. These were regulars, and many of them were standing around and socializing with each other for 20 minutes straight.

I continued my workout, turning my attention to the weights. I got laser-focused on the task at hand, nothing else. I was in the middle of a tremendous lift, when suddenly a commercial came blaring over the loudspeaker, interrupting the "workout music" with this sales message (not verbatim): "Sometimes you're just too busy to do everything you need to do. We understand! So for times like that, we offer our members in good standing the ability to put their account on hold! And you can come back to your membership at a later date when circumstances permit! Some restrictions apply. See your helpful fitness center representative for details!"

I finished my workout as quick as I could. I went home and immediately charged my iPod.

This is a true story. As it turns out, the fitness center plays the same audio program all the time, I had just never listened to it before. And also of note: Almost every person in the gym who was actually working out and physically fit *was wearing headphones.*

But what about the other people there? Did they *want* to get healthy and strong? Yes, of course they did or they wouldn't be there. Does standing around and socializing while leaning on a piece of exercise equipment and listening to love songs make people healthy and strong? Easy question – the answer is no.

So apparently there was something directing the actions of these people, and it wasn't their fitness goals. And remember, this was the *majority* of the people (social agreement!!). And not just *any* people – these were people who actually have a gym membership, and actually show up at a gym. So close to success, inches away, but something trips them up.

I can truly tell you that life's circumstances occur very differently for the successful than for those who fail. Having had ample experience in both ways of living, I have experienced this difference for myself. When I made the switch from *wanting* success to *having* success in various areas of my life, I suddenly found myself being asked all kinds of questions about what it takes to get there. "How do I get strong and healthy?" "How can I have better relationships?" "How can I create wealth in my life?" What's interesting is that many of the people who were asking these questions had the same information I did. After thinking about it, I let them know that my success has come from simply following through on what I said I was going to do, and doing it consistently.

Now if that last statement seems obvious to you, congratulations, you are someone who has your eyes open and is willing to confront reality. Whenever I've been in conversation with other high-achieving people about the difference between the "haves" and the "have-nots" of this world, and what it would take for an individual to stop wanting success and actually experience it, this idea has come up.

As we saw in our grocery store and fitness center examples, all the people there had the same resources, but had vastly different results. The successful person, therefore, must have some additional ingredient. "Perhaps it's a great secret... They must know something that they're not telling everyone else!!" As amusing as this sounds to any successful person, and as moronic as those examples might seem, there is a very real and vital ingredient missing in the lives of those who fail. It can be found in the title of this book.

You see, there's perfect integrity in the universe. It will never fail you. If you jump off a building, you will always go down. If you stick your finger in a light bulb socket, you are going to get shocked. If you pound sugar down your throat and go to the gym to socialize, you are going to get fat. If you waste your days working a job you don't like, you are going to get broke and miserable. Here's the thing: These are all choices you can make, or not make! The question is, who's making the choices?

There is a saying: to know the truth and the truth will set you free. "Free from what?" some may ask. Free from ignorance! Freedom from ignorance is the greatest freedom there is. The problem with most people is they don't know who they are. They don't know that they are powerful. Often, they don't even know what they want. How then could they act with integrity to themselves? They can't. If you don't have YOU, you don't have anything - you've got no shot at success. Whoever coined the phrase "ignorance is bliss" must have been living on another planet.

Nothing is more terrible than ignorance in action.
Johann Wolfgang von Goethe (1749 – 1832)

How do you think guys like Donald Trump can come back after major financial upset? He knew who he was. And his knowingness was independent of the bank statement. He was Donald Trump, regardless of what some ink on a piece of paper said.

And on the subject of money, how many people really know who they are in relationship to money? Most people think they have to work for money, as if money is the master and they are its servant. That's not who you are. You are the master, and money is your servant. It's a tool for you to use to carry out your intentions, provide service and build wealth through businesses, investing and educating yourself. You're in the director's chair. And by recognizing that you're in the director's chair you can be more powerful and deliberate in your ability to attract those pieces of paper that are going to go to work for you. But it's not going to happen by thinking that *you've* got to work for *them*.

Imagine the great Stephen Spielberg, sitting in his director's chair; but instead of creating a masterpiece, he's asking the cameraman if he thinks it would be okay to make the action movie he planned, or maybe they should just change the whole project and do a movie about... love and ponies. And then the gaffer comes over and tells Stephen that he wants some coffee, "So stop whatever it is you're doing now and go get me some coffee, because my mouth is getting a little dry over here." And then, while Stephen the director is out getting coffee, one of the sound crew approaches him and tells him that he really hasn't been very good at getting the coffee, and that the last time he got coffee for her it was cold. So he is going to have to step it up, maybe put in some overtime.

Now this is a ridiculous example, but hopefully you got a visual of someone who completely forgot their role. They were in the director's chair, but now they're being bossed around by stage-hands. This is what our relationship with money looks like when we're confused about its purpose.

One of the first things that I had to do to get this relationship straight was to put myself in the moment and remember who I am. Right now, meaning *right now*, meaning in this exact moment, what would be different in my life if my bank statement had some different ink on it? Here I am, I'm standing here, I didn't lose an arm or a leg, I'm doing well. The ink on paper doesn't seem to be affecting my present reality in any way. The moment that I acknowledge my independence I am able to free up some energy that I was wasting on fear and start putting it into creative thinking. I can come up with some ideas about how to put myself in a bigger, better director's chair, to create some more flow, some more abundance to live the lifestyle that I say I want to live (a life of choices). And that was totally impossible for me to do when I was giving away all my power to this symbol, this ink on paper, this idea that so many people feel like they are at the effect of.

Know who you are. Be that. Do it now. Do it consistently. When people don't do this they are no longer at cause in their life, and they are subject to the superstitions and excuses that other outer-directed people want to sell them. (Like it's okay to stand around and socialize, or put your gym membership on hold because you've got circumstances.) People who live at the effect of their circumstances seem to demand that others do so as well. A person who's demonstrating ineffectiveness in their life would rather create a story to justify it than consider how they are creating it.

Again, let's think about how this relates to money. At the time of this writing, most people are broke. So there's a superstition around it. And where does superstition come from? It comes from ignorance. Most people's experience with money is like a caveman's experience of fire: There is very little of it. There is some mystical process that you have to go through to get any of it going in your life. Others are going to come and steal it from you. You've got to fight over it. It's yours, your fire, and if it's yours it can't be theirs. It's difficult to acquire. Only a few can have the experience of it, because they are stronger and better (they know how to do the special magic rock and stick trick). Yeah, most people's experience of money is not highly evolved.

Then come the excuses and justifications. "Money won't make you happy." Now, I agree with that if we're talking about sports cars, the over-eating of excessively rich dinners every night, insatiable consumerism, and being obsessed with our possessions. Of course I agree that money won't make you happy. Things don't have the power over people to make them happy. The equation doesn't even make sense. But if we're talking about having options and freedom in our life? I'll tell you what...the ability to serve, the ability to choose how I spend my days, the ability to be a contributor to society - to educate people who are living in ignorance, the ability to take time off from my typical business activities and hang out in a cabin by the creek to write this book... yeah, that makes me happy. Knowing that I'm free, knowing that I have options in my life makes me happy. Money will buy you that. Let's stop making excuses for being broke.

So there is a perfect cycle of thought, feeling, action and result happening everywhere we look. And we can regain a lot of energy if we're aware of this. Now I can choose to recognize that for myself and for others. And I can choose to forgive myself and others for having missed the mark, and having perfectly demonstrated poor results. Even if it was a perfect demonstration of "I'm such a victim. I love to struggle. My word doesn't mean shit." That's all in the past. I get to decide who I'm being *now*, and it doesn't take long to transform one's experience. My story proves that. How does one do this?

Imagine that each day you had a blank piece of paper on which you could draw or write anything you wanted. It's a magical paper, bequeathed unto you by the gods, and whatever you put on it will shape the events and circumstances in your life that day. Certainly, we would have some ideas of what we would like to see based on our past experiences, but the point to remember is that the paper is blank when we get it at the beginning of the day. There is no precedent set by yesterday's performance or results. It is completely blank. And as tempting as it may be to base our drawing on who we were yesterday, it is totally unnecessary to do so. In fact, it is only by clinging to yesterday that such a self-limiting error could be committed again and again. It is only by abandoning my attachment to the past, by forgiving my past completely, that I get to entertain new possibilities.

Let the weak say, I am strong.
Joel 3:10

This willingness to press the "Reset Button" on one's experience is a vital factor in accelerating one's progress in life. If not for this, we would simply reenact outworn programs of ineffectiveness. People will continue to struggle if they continue to cling to a self-image program that is based on their past, instead of their possibilities. And they will continue to struggle if they look to the guy next to them to see what they "should" expect out of life, because "everyone else is doing it".

This is our starting point - a blank piece of paper. Or maybe it's a plank of wood. The difference between the successful and the unsuccessful is one's willingness to be at cause. Are your thoughts at cause for moving you into high-integrity action so you can live the life you choose? Or are your thoughts at the effect of appearances, opinions, superstitions, neuroses and ignorance, reinforced by the masses who would rather make excuses than win at life?

I'm here to say that *you* are already in possession of the most vital elements for *your* success. But that doesn't help you if you don't know who you are. "Know Thyself" is not a new idea, and because of its simplicity the masses who habitually dramatize failure disregard it. That doesn't mean that you have to participate in their collective ignorance.

So what does success look like for you? What is it that *you* want? What experiences would you prefer to have accompanying you on this journey of life? And are you willing to do what it takes to have them?

Think about this: the price of success is not greater than the price of failure. I would say that the price of success is less than the price of failure. The price of success you pay once, the price of failure you pay over and over and over again. Which is the bigger price - proper nutrition and consistent exercise, or walking around in a less-than-able body enslaved by lethargy and obesity? What's the bigger price - becoming diligent in your business activities or living in poverty and always making excuses for why you do? What's the bigger price - fidelity in your relationships and being a person of your word, or living a life of ruined relationships, ultimately leading to loneliness and lacking the respect of your fellow man? I say that success is the lesser price, but you have to choose.

-Simple Action-

Three Part Personal Inventory: Get a notebook or journal, start with page one and write today's date on top, along with the current time. Describe where you feel you are in terms of your personal success up to this point. You are simply identifying a stepping-off point from this time forward. It need not be long, although it could be. The point is to be honest with yourself. Include actions that are obviously not serving you. For example:

Eat fast-food three times a day;

Don't call my client back for two days;

Argue with my spouse over money and whatever else, etc.

Once this is done, go to page two and write the date and time on top. (This should be the same date as page one, with a slightly later time.) Write down some *simple* statements to describe experiences that you would like to begin causing in your life immediately. For example:

Strong body;

Happy relationship;

Vacation fund, etc.

Then, identify some simple (not complicated) actions you could immediately engage in that would move you in the direction of the pleasing experiences you've identified. For example:

Do at least 20 minutes of physically demanding exercise per day;

Eat raw or lightly cooked green vegetables with at least 2 meals per day;

Read at least 10 pages per day of an empowering book or subject of interest;

Walk with family after dinner, etc.

At the end of each day, go back to your journal and make a list of some high-integrity activities you did that day. They may seem simple or they may seem profound; the point is that you acknowledge yourself for what you did right – *you did what you said you were going to do*.

The following two steps are optional but recommended:

Go back to page one and tear it out of the journal. Destroy it using some auspicious, ceremonial method. Fire is a popular choice here. Be creative and have fun. And remember that the only property to be destroyed is that piece of paper, specifically.

Get a clean piece of copy-machine paper. Hang it on the wall in your office or some other relevant place. Let it remind you of your future. Let it also be a conversation piece. If anyone should inadvertently write something on it or mark it in any way, make the big investment and get a new piece of paper.

ON A MISSION

To get better results in our life we must depart from the ways of the masses. And to do that we are going to have to question some of our beliefs, if not many of our beliefs. And this can be scary, because many people have been conditioned to believe that they are not even worthy of questioning their beliefs. So this takes guts. People who get results are people of courage. I say to people when they come to me for business training that I am not here to baby-sit the weak. I am here to assist people who are already successful in their mind, who have already predetermined that they are going to create results in their life. I'm here to show them how to save themselves some time, how to accelerate the process. If you've been conned into believing that you are a weak and helpless person, or at worst, that you're not even worthy of questioning who you are or your beliefs, then I can't help you. Nobody can help you. The first thing that we've got to do is be willing to take a look.

For me, a lot of this conditioning originally came from organized religion. Being "a child of God" was just a platitude that nobody really believed in, that I could tell. When you're surrounded by people who walk around like cattle it's difficult to imagine that you could be powerful. But get around people who are going somewhere in life and you'll find that they are an inner-directed group. They decide what they want, they decide who they are, and they go to any lengths to get it.

You know that most people don't even know what they want? Every day I have an opportunity to talk with people in my business affairs. I have an opportunity to talk with people who say that they want increase in their life, greater abundance, more money. But when asked what the money is for they don't have an answer - maybe a lot of ambiguity. Some people say they want to be their own boss, some people say they want to earn a little extra money so they can just survive a little bit more comfortably, which is such a copout, such a compromise. The people who I found are on the path of greatness and who have achieved great things are people who know exactly what they want and are willing to go to any lengths to get it. They play to win. Now, if we don't know what we want, how can we play to win? Most people play to *not lose*, if they play at all. Most people spend 90% of their energy maintaining mediocrity and 10% at best of their thought energy goes into future possibilities, because they have no concrete future possibilities. All they know is maintaining mediocrity and compromise. So they can't even get into the game.

What successful people do is they reverse the equation. Let's put 90% of our energy into our possibilities (and we know what these possibilities are). Here are the things that I've decided that I will experience in my life. And I'm going to put 90% of my energy into that, and the other 10% I can put into maintaining what is practically running on autopilot anyway – standard-issue activities of daily survival. But when you're in the thick of it, when you're in the thick of survival, knowing that it takes almost 100% of your energy just to maintain what isn't enough already, it's difficult for a lot of people to make that shift. What we must do is fill our minds with possibilities. We must seek examples that inspire us to create goals of our own. Having these goals, and taking new action towards them, leads to creating new habits which will supplant the old habits that have ensured our lasting mediocrity.

We can not simply abandon a habitual way of thinking without replacing it with a new one. We cannot abandon a habitual way of behavior without replacing it with a new one. There are very few voids in the universe. The only one that I can think of at this moment is a black hole. And since you're not a black hole, know that there is not going to be a void in your life. Something will come in to fill that void. So we must make preparation to fill the void of our old habits with new habits, and it can happen very quickly, but it's not going to happen if we haven't decided on a destination.

Let's say that you want to become wealthy. And you decide that your first goal on your way to wealth will be to earn $10,000 per month. If you were speaking to me about this personally the first thing that I would ask you is "What's the $10,000 per month for?" There has to be a *why*. There has to be a reason, a significant reason, significant for you. It has to mean something for *you*. It's not enough to say, "I want $10,000 per month." There has to be emotion involved. Logical goals are not inspirational goals.

Now, I know this defies generations of experts who have been giving you advice, and I'm okay with that. Let me break the news to you: it's easier to earn $50,000 per month (if that's what you truly want) than it is to earn what you're probably earning at your job. Why is that? Because, when people are motivated by something that they really want, they get on a mission. It is no longer a job, it is a quest. If we were to approach earning $10,000 per month from the viewpoint of the logical and reasonable person, we would start with a plan of logistics, very left-brain, with not much flexibility. And yet, our great good lies in the realm of uncertainty. And many brilliant teachers have taught us this. If we already knew how to reach our goals, we would have already reached them! So it's imperative that we step outside of our comfort zone, outside of our logic zone, and get into the realm of uncertainty. Are you ready to take action in the realm of uncertainty? Of course, the answer is no. Guess what? Nobody is.

But will you move into action anyway? It's simple logic that this is what high-achieving people have done to make their mark in life. The most outrageously successful people I have ever met or worked with have the least attachment to their comfort zone. The world knows them as *leaders*. They are the few.

So if someone asks me, "John, what does it really take to succeed?" I could simply say, "To be a leader." And what does it mean to be a leader? To have a destination in your life. To have vision. As a pretty smart guy named Solomon said:

Where there is no vision, the people perish.
Proverbs 29:18

A leader is a person with vision. In other words, they have a visual picture of where they are going. They have a *guaranteed future outcome*. It is an unshakable purpose. It is an attitude that says. "I will not be denied!"

Let's face it, who wants to follow someone who isn't going anywhere? And since all our opportunities come through other people (not from, but *through*), it would be imperative to have a vision that we can enroll other people in, or that they enroll themselves in. In my years in business, I have seen so many people with good intentions miss the mark because they never developed the vision of a leader. The essential "knowingness" that magnetizes others to you. This is indispensable. There have been so many books written on the subject of leadership that it boggles the mind. Some of the information is good. Most of it unnecessarily complicates the subject.

The simple fact is, a leader is a person with a destination. A deliberately chosen, self-determined destination. It's just as simple as that. These people with specific vision find themselves almost automatically succeeding in whatever endeavors they are engaged in. People are drawn to them and they find themselves with partnerships and affiliations that are synergistic and require less effort than may be expected.

I could, and I have, spent countless hours counseling people who, for whatever reason, did not grasp the basic essence of leadership as I just laid out here. And because they lacked vision for themselves, any "how-to" type advice that I could give them was ineffective. For people to be effective, they must first have the vision. I could spend the next 20 pages of this book saying that over and over and over again, because it is so vital. I have come to believe that when the vision is there, the how-to virtually takes care of itself. But when the vision is not there, the how-to doesn't matter.

There are also many books these days, directing people to what I call "quick-fix" systematized approaches to success. And while I believe in systems, they do not negate the fact that people must still operate their systems effectively. In the field of business, we must remember that people buy from people. So many people have attempted to automate themselves right out of their own business through the promise of some system that will supposedly do all their "work" for them. And while systems work to save us time and make us more effective, there must still be a leader at the helm steering the ship.

Quick-fix approaches to parenting and relationships have been equally fruitless. I don't believe you can run a communication formula on someone and have it be effective, because some expert said so. In the area of human relationships, authenticity is what people respond to. People want to be heard. People want to know that they are actually in communication with someone. There is an old saying, "people don't care how much you know, until they know how much you care."

Again, let's remember that all of our opportunities come through other people. Therefore, leadership, which is a skill that any diligent person can develop, should be a primary focus. So what does it take to do this? Again I say, a leader is a person of vision. The leader has a destination in their life. As I indicated before, I like to think of it as a "guaranteed future outcome." There is no question about where we're going, and we know we're going to get there. And with this vision, others are enrolled. So let's craft our vision.

Suppose you are the owner or the primary decision-maker of a company. I always like talking to entrepreneurs because they understand the urgency of developing a vision for themselves and their associates. And let's say you have a goal of earning $500,000 for yourself within the next year. For you to accomplish this, you must have effectiveness in your business organization. And since leadership starts from the top, it starts with you. So here's the big question: What's the money for? The answer to this cannot be a vague one. For a person with no experience in wealth creation, this may seem like a major disconnect. What does it matter to the organization what the leader wants to earn money for this year? But make no mistake about it, it's of paramount importance. Not to the individuals themselves, but to their ability to be enrolled in the vision of their leader.

My recommendation to this person would be to set what some people have referred to as "SMART goals." SMART is an acronym that stands for Specific, Measurable, Achievable, Relevant and Timely.

Specific:
This person wants to be able to provide a lifestyle for themselves and their family. Success in their business means

they will be able to send their children to the schools of their choice. They will be able to take the family on that vacation that they've been thinking about for however long. And they've had their eye on that new BMW sedan with the monster engine and amenities that didn't exist just a couple of years ago (the silver one with the beige leather interior). For some reason it just keeps showing up on their radar. Whatever the reasons are to make the money, it's *their* reasons, and therefore they are good reasons to make the money.

Now, pay close attention to this part. This person may have some outstanding debt, some "previous obligations" that they must also take care of. But this cannot be the primary focus of their goal. Any person of integrity will, of course, take care of their previous obligations, but they will do so in the process of getting what it is that they really want. To focus on debt is complete futility, because, as so many of the greatest thinkers in the history of our planet have taught us, we get what we focus on. The bottom line is, the money is already spent in our minds. We have a specific use for the money in advance. We have a reason to earn the money, and it is a specific one.

Measurable:
$500,000 is what it will cost to fulfill the intention. It is a quantifiable amount that is in direct correlation with the products and services that motivate the leader. Simple as that.

Achievable:
This is a goal that is believable to the individual. Perhaps it's a large jump up from their previous earnings and lifestyle, but it's one that's believable to them. At the same time, it should not be a goal that is based on what we have already accomplished in the past. So many people base their expectations for their future

on their past performance or their past level of effectiveness. Please make note of this. The past brings *no precedent* to what we may expect of ourselves today. So long as it is believable in the mind of the person setting the goal, and at the same time stretches them beyond what they've done before, it is a worthy ideal. Perhaps they do not know the specifics of how it will all come together. And that's okay! No one knows how to reach their goal until they've reached it. Note that if we fail to create the vision, then the goal will never be reached. So we have to start with the vision. More will be revealed in terms of "how-to", as we begin to take action.

Relevant:

This goal must be of significant emotional relevance to the individual. This is perhaps the most important part of goal setting. I heard someone once say, "Logical salespeople have skinny kids." The question we can ask ourselves is not "What do I think?", but "How do I feel?" The key word here is emotion. "How does that make me feel once I reach that goal?" Again, we cannot be vague. I recommend that people sit down and get quiet for some time and see themselves already in possession of the money and the good that they seek, and that they do this to the extent that they actually begin to feel the feelings that will be theirs once the goal is accomplished. And then do it some more. And then do it again. This is a very powerful exercise to do. So often, I speak with people who have logical goals, goals that are reasonable, but carry no inspiration. When I ask them what it would be like to accomplish that goal, they say something like "great". Terribly vague. The goal should be something that motivates the individual beyond logic. It has to be relevant to them - *them specifically*. Not their spouse, not their children, not anyone else. Even though these others may be an intrinsic part of the goal, the person setting the goal is the one it must be relevant to, because it's *their* goal! No one can set your goal for you and you cannot set a goal for anyone else. This may sound selfish to the person who is new at goal setting, but it's not selfish at all. It's just the way it works. In fact, the most selfish thing this person could do is to *not* set a goal and to subsequently fail, thereby subjecting their spouse, children etc. to failure lifestyle. To become personally successful is the most *unselfish* thing this person could do, because not only does it give them the means to provide the lifestyle for themselves and their loved ones, but it also sets an example of success and self-reliance, which is so rare and so required today.

Timely:

We must set a deadline. Without this, we are subject to the endless demands of every day life that scream for our attention. There will always be something more urgent - not more important - but more urgent than reaching your goals. Sometimes our goals require us to radically alter how we choose to spend our time. But again we're not talking about staying in our comfort zone of what we already know how to accomplish. Our worthy goal requires our willingness to make adjustments. Sometimes we have to extricate ourselves from habits that no longer serve us. Setting deadlines gives us a roadmap to do this. And keep in mind, the date that we set for the completion of our goal is a guess. It may be an educated guess, but it's still a guess. Very few people have a fully operational crystal ball that will reveal the exact time of completion for every intention that they commit to. What's interesting is that most people give themselves more time than is necessary for the fulfillment of their goal, because again, they're expectations are based on their past experiences. Be willing to be bold. The greatest leaders I've known have always known that they were going to reach every goal that they set for themselves, regardless of the time that it took to complete them. So tighten it up. Create some urgency. Work expands to fill the time allowed for it! Read that last line again. How long do you want it to take? If you reach your goal early will you be upset? If you miss it by a few days or weeks, would you have been happier had you not reached the goal at all? I don't think so. So make an educated guess and get to work.

Once we have completely identified the goal. The next step is to write it down. This is an activity that approximately 3% of people do. And isn't it interesting that it's about 3% of our population (at best) that can be considered high achievers. There was a university study years ago, that surveyed the effectiveness people who wrote down their goals, compared to those who did not. 3% of the people had written goals, and 97% did not. After some time, it was revealed that the real-world results of the people with written goals exceeded the combined results of the entire group of people without specific written goals. So this apparently works.

And why does it work? There are several reasons. One is obvious - that we get what we think about. Certainly, a person who is focused on a vision is giving mental energy to that vision much more than a person who does not have a specific vision written down to remind them on a consistent basis of where they're going. Another reason that this works is that we're bringing our mental picture into the physical realm. This may sound a bit esoteric, but think about it. When I write down a goal, I have brought thought energy from the ether into my physical world. I am actually proving to myself that I can manifest in my physical world something that has come from the plane of thought, the "no-thing." The field of pure potentiality and infinite possibilities.

And isn't this how everything that we know in our life has been created? The building we live in was nothing but an idea in the mind of the person who was about to build it at one time. We have an idea about our ideal spouse or partner, and those kinds of people begin to show up in our lives. Thomas Edison had a vision of illuminating the world with electricity, and now we only burn candles and oil lamps for nostalgia or aromatherapy.

When we write the goal we take the key points from the five components that we just identified and make a concise statement, written in the present tense, that will consistently remind us of where we're going. I like to carry a goal card with me wherever I go as a reminder. If this is a new idea for you, know that this has been working for centuries, probably for as long as there has been paper or stone tablets small enough to fit in the fur pocket of the caveman who wanted a bigger and better cave for his cavewoman and cave children.

It may go something like this:

By day/month/year.
I feel so confident, grateful and empowered now that I earn $500,000 per year, by providing the best service possible in the capacity of _____. My children have enrolled in _____ school and we have booked our family trip to Italy. I drive a new BMW 760Li, silver with beige leather interior and all the options. I feel totally carefree about everything in my life including money. I know I deserve this and even more.

All bases have been covered. Specific, measurable, achievable, relevant and timely. It's brief. It fits on a small card in your pocket that's with you wherever you go. It includes words that are powerful for you, and it can be rewritten every time you visualize a more detailed and specific image that brings new and more vivid emotions that would warrant a rewriting.

I debated with myself about whether or not I would include this SMART goals formula and goal card technique in this book, because it seems so basic to me and I feel like I've heard it a million times. But I did include it, because most people's results (97%) would indicate that they haven't heard it, or if they did, that they aren't applying it. In fact, an interesting thing has happened for me as a byproduct of using this technique and teaching it to others. This is a great time-saver, and it can be used by anyone who is managing an organization of people who are working to improve their lives – in other words, anyone who isn't passing their days punching a clock at a repetitious and obligatory job. If I am ever speaking with someone who wants to tell me about their circumstances and how they are struggling with such-and-such, I can end the conversation and avoid becoming the person who is cosigning their helplessness by asking this one question: "What does your goal card say?" They never, never, never know it! Interesting.

Obstacles are those frightful things you see when you take your eyes off your goals.
Henry Ford (1863 – 1947)

This goal card is a tool to consistently re-stimulate our vision. Every time we feel it in our pocket or elsewhere (I know a very successful woman who keeps hers in her bra) we are reminded of where we're going. And that visualization includes the emotional state of having accomplished the goal.

There is much talk these days about visualization and affirmation and the like. Visualization is a great tool when you operate it properly, and it can be quite lame when you don't. The breakthrough that I've had in the area of visualization is one of relationship. Now listen to this. In my life I have relationships with various people - common relationships, casual relationships - my friends, my wife, relatives, etc. These are people that I have conversations with, some on a more regular basis than others. These are people that I know. I know their way of talking. I know their facial expressions. I know how they occur in my life. I have a mental image of how they are in my life.

So when I'm visualizing a goal, I have found that it's most powerful to visualize my interaction with these people who I have already existing relationships with, who I can speak with in a very casual, conversational way. I visualize myself having a conversation with them, one that I will have once I have accomplished what my intention is. I see myself occurring in their life, interacting with them as the person who has already accomplished whatever the intention is. This has been the most powerful visualization for me because it brings relationships into it. It brings my relationship with other people, which is something I'm constantly and consistently involved with, into this new idea, this reality that I'm manifesting in my life. This has been the most powerful way of visualizing for me. Include conversations with other people in your visualizations, feel the emotions which come from that, and it will accelerate the process beautifully.

Finally, I think any leader of our day would agree that they sometimes feel like Columbus on a quest for the New World.

Despite the naysayers, critics, circumstances, suppressive people, etc. we find fuel for action in our vision, and we hold our course, knowing what we know.

Great spirits have always encountered violent opposition from mediocre minds. The mediocre mind is incapable of understanding the man who refuses to bow blindly to conventional prejudices and chooses instead to express his opinions courageously and honestly.
Albert Einstein (1879 – 1955)

If you're a leader in your chosen field you must decide right now to never allow other people to sell you their belief systems. This will take a leader down more thoroughly than anything I've seen in my personal life. My results soar (financially and otherwise) when I'm independent of the belief systems of others. And when I allow someone else to sell me their belief system, my results have plummeted. I don't even look sideways to see what other people are doing. I'm very deliberate about the energy that I allow to enter into my mind.

Some of this is very subtle. People like to send me clippings from news articles and e-mail posts and this sort of stuff. (Oh look, here's some more negativity about *this*. But did you hear about this unfortunate incident that happened to this person? They are such a victim.) There are a lot of "drama-queens" on this planet. I used to be one. If you're finding yourself in an environment that doesn't empower you, immediately choose a different environment or take proactive steps to transform that environment as expeditiously as possible. We get like the people we surround ourselves with. I don't know anyone who's immune to this. Why do you think monks spent so much time in solitude and silence?

Choosing to walk the path of the few will take understanding and responsibility. I'd like to make a distinction here because many people have a completely erroneous idea about leadership and how that shows up in the lives of others.

In speaking of leaders, I'm not talking about a tyrannical type of personality, a dominating, domineering person, someone who induces fear in their subordinates, or anything like this. And I'm also not talking about someone who's engaged in shameless self-promotion and who wants to take the credit for everything (although a leader does take responsibility).

What I'm talking about is the best leaders, people that induce others to be the best that they can be. When in the company of a person like this, and there are very few of them, we find that the people who are on their team have the feeling that they are achieving great accomplishments *themselves*; that they are not a subordinate of the leader, but that they are leading alongside the leader. The leader has the vision, and the leader enrolls these other leaders (who are leading alongside) in their vision. So we have people that are not being held down, but that are also developing their self-reliance and becoming leaders themselves. This is what I mean by true leadership.

If I accept you as you are, I will make you worse; however if I treat you as though you are what you are capable of becoming, I help you become that.
Johann Wolfgang von Goethe (1749 – 1832)

-Simple Action-

Don't leave home without a goal card on your person. Don't go to sleep tonight without having made one. Review this vision/goal often throughout the day. Rewrite as necessary.

Subscribe to magazines that enhance your vision of where you're going in your life. For example: fitness magazines, luxury-lifestyle magazines, homes and architecture, hobbies and activities of specific interest to you, etc.

THREE MAGIC WORDS

Picture this: You're sitting on the sofa and you're thinking about that new action/adventure film that was just released on DVD. You haven't seen it yet because you never made it to the theaters while it was playing there. Suddenly, the front door swings open and your spouse walks in with that very DVD in hand! Hooray. You make popcorn. You fire up the widescreen display and the sound system. You dim the lights.

Your spouse puts the DVD into the player. Everyone's ready to witness the intrigue, the suspense, the spectacle of this blockbuster film. The disc navigation menu is on-screen, and the holder of the remote control selects the *final chapter* of the movie. It begins playing, and everyone watches the triumphant conclusion of this tale of bravery and heroism. The villain is defeated, the princess is saved, etc.

Wow, that was exciting. Now it's time for a bathroom break, but there's no need to pause the movie, because it's over. Afterwards, you come back and decide to watch the remainder of the movie, from the beginning forward. As you do, you are introduced to a whole cast of characters, the protagonist, the antagonist, etc. Various situations occur which try the courage of our hero. He barely escapes death several times. But through all of it, you know he will be victorious because you already saw the end of the movie. The cat's out of the bag. You watch the drama unfold now with a quiet detachment because you know of the guaranteed future outcome which must occur.

You *know* the hero is going to slay the dragon. You know all the adversity is going to work out in his favor. You cheer him on as he considers backing down in fear as he faces his adversary. There is no need for him to hesitate, he *will* win this battle, even though he just got beat up pretty bad in the last scene. It doesn't matter. He has to win. It is his purpose to win, and the only thing he can do is win. Apparently he knows this and moves into action…

A major difference that I have found between people who *want* success, and those who get on with success, who reap the rewards they intend, is that successful people are willing to act, even before they are 100% prepared. There is a boldness that would indicate a great deal of necessity, or a belief that success is pre-ordained. This may seem unreasonable, and of course, one thing that we can never accuse highly successful people of being is *reasonable*.

The reasonable man adapts himself to the world: the unreasonable one persists in trying to adapt the world to himself. Therefore all progress depends on the unreasonable man.
George Bernard Shaw (1856 – 1950)

I have never met one person who was content with their circumstances who was also motivated to make a change in their life. People sometimes have to be right up against the wall for them to be motivated enough to take actions that are outside of their comfort zone. Because, after all, who likes change? When I look at my own life, I can see clearly how I used to deify my comfort zone. Hanging on to the little bit of so-called security that I had in my life. It was that little bit of certainty that I could rely on in my own pathetic, mediocre existence which cost me most of my energy. Maintaining mediocrity is a lot of work.

I had very little energy to put into my goals, and I had no certainty about my ability to reach my goals. Sure, I had desires of increase, abundance and success, but my life was about maintaining with all my might the little bit that I had.

And this is poverty consciousness in the purest sense. I can not go to the next plateau in my life while maintaining the previous plateau. In other words, I have to be like the trapeze artists at the circus who must release one trapeze bar to be able to reach the next bar. It comes down to faith; a knowingness that I am here to succeed.

I do myself no good by living in a comfort zone, avoiding the inevitable changes of life until my back is right against the wall. It doesn't have to be this way. What I can choose to know, and what I can choose to remember, is that the reason I have these great desires motivating me in my life is because I am meant to have these desires fulfilled in my life. And when I doubt this, I find myself clinging to so-called security. But the reality of the situation is that security does not come from my current circumstances. It does not come from money. It does not come from a paycheck given to me by a boss at a job. My security comes from knowing that I am willing to take the actions necessary to fulfill my intention. That is where it has always come from.

I made a decision years ago that I would make an example of myself, that I would break the pattern of poverty consciousness I witnessed for most of my young life, and become an example of what is possible if people would become willing to act. Where did I get the motivation for that? Some have called it "divine dissatisfaction." While other people may accept mediocrity as "their lot in life", I was unwilling to do that. I will not be denied the desire *that is seeking me at least as much as I am seeking it*. And because success is what I sought, success is what I found. "Seek and ye shall find" is a true statement!

But what about my circumstances? But what about reality? For as long as I based my decisions on my circumstances I remained in the prison of ignorance, in denial of my own power and living at the effect of the outer world. And yes, I know we all have circumstances. Many people have struggled, or are struggling, with uncongenial situations and tragedies in their life, but if we believe even a word of the great masters who have all given us the same truth throughout the history of our planet, then we must consider that *we really do* shape our circumstances by our habitual patterns of thought. So what does this mean? This means I have to use my will. Now I'm not talking about willpower the way most people understand it. Many people have a misunderstanding of this idea of will - the mental faculty of will. This is one of the intellectual factors that separate us from our house pets and the animals of the world. The purpose of the will - the reason we have the mental faculty of will - is this and only this: TO CHOOSE THE RIGHT THOUGHT.

A man cannot directly choose his circumstances, but he can choose his thoughts, and so indirectly, yet surely, shape his circumstances.
James Allen (1864 – 1912)

That's it. There is no other proper use for the will. It is not to force oneself to take actions that they really don't want to take. It is not to quit some counterproductive activity. It is not to force yourself to stop procrastinating. It is to choose the right thoughts consistently enough, and often enough, that it begins to shape our self image. We become the person we really want to be. Then we take the actions *that* person would take, and instantly we begin attracting circumstances in our life that are in alignment with our vision. Again, this takes faith. This requires an understanding of one of the most basic principles of creating what you want. It is something I never get tired of talking about at my seminars and on my teleconferences. It is known as the BE DO HAVE principle. This has taken me from years of hypothesizing and theorizing and philosophizing about success, to actually experiencing success. These three words in this exact order: BE DO HAVE. If you get only three words out of this whole book, let it be these three. To the extent that you embody this concept, you are unstoppable. Let's take it from the top.

BEING

All doing is preceded by being. People who seem to be lucky or have the Midas touch - "everything that they touch turns to gold" - are those who are thoroughly *being* in the flow, and are thoroughly *being* people of success, with no counter-intention. These are the people who seem to take the spontaneous right action that brings them fortunate results. And the reason that they seem to take spontaneous right action is because they *are* taking spontaneous right action.

Conversely, the person who seems to always struggle - the person who is not experiencing the flow of life - they are a person who seems to make the wrong decision quite often, and this can also be attributed to who they are *being*.

In my business trainings, I naturally have people asking me every conceivable question about the "how-to" of business. "What kind of advertising should I do?" "What do I say when my prospective customer says this?" "How often should I send out the e-mail?" "Why is the sky blue?" "Is it okay to urinate in the shower?" Etc. But all the how-to in the world isn't going to bear fruit for someone who is not first being the person who would have the result.

Wallace Wattles in his classic book "The Science of Getting Rich" spoke of doing things in a certain way. Two people engaged in the same activity can have completely different results, because it's not the activities themselves, but the certain way that they are doing them that gets a pleasing result. And, of course, to do things in a certain way requires that we think in a certain way. This way of thinking would indicate *that we've become that person who would have the result* that is pleasing to us. We then operate our lives and take action *from that position*. If not, we struggle because we can never outperform our self image. Forcing doesn't work.

Beingness is a primary state to manifesting what it is that you would have in your life. It is the primary area of focus for anyone who is going to a higher level of expression in their life. And we can cultivate this beingness in a very simple way. The way is by choosing the right thoughts. When we do this consistently and deliberately it results in an elevated emotional state. That state becomes part of our self-image, our beingness.

You see, to identify who we are being, our innermost beliefs about who we are and what we're capable of and what we're expecting in our lives, we can ask ourselves one question, and that is "How do I feel?"

"How do I feel?" is the question. The answer to that question will reveal who I am being very reliably. So if I'm happy and peaceful and confident and having fun, then that's who I'm being. I'm a person who is in that flow, and the currents of life, including the currency of the wallet and the bank account, flows to me with no force.

But if I'm stressed out, anxious, pissed-off, resentful - then that's who I'm being. I'm a person who's going against the flow. I'm a person who's cutting off the currents in my life, who's short-circuiting my own energy. And, once again, we can never outperform our self-image. By being this person, all the hard work in the world isn't going to bring me satisfaction. All the trying (and I get that there are a lot of people that are trying really hard to be successful) will not bear fruit. *You can't be successful until you become successful!*

Think about this. Most people think that success comes from having already gotten the result, having already completed the project, having already lost the weight, having already made the money, having already landed the big deal. But that's attachment to appearances. That's what most people do. All the people that I've ever met who are working their life away at an ordinary job (we are talking about the "sheeple" of life) think that once they do the job good enough for long enough, then they may get the promotion. They may get a commendation or some sort of recognition from an authority figure, then ultimately they'll have credibility or the belief that they are successful. That's how to give all your power away to some outside phenomenon, in this case your boss or your job. This is how to give one's responsibility for who they are being away to their life circumstances. And it's terribly disempowering. People spend countless years going nowhere in a job because they are never good enough. They are constantly deferring a life of possibility and a life of choice for some imagined retirement day.

No, the self-reliant person, the entrepreneurial type person, is a person who says, "You know what, I'm credible now. I'm successful now." Because what does it mean to be successful? My favorite definition of success is *the progressive realization of a worthy ideal.* That was the definition that Earl Nightingale made people aware of years ago in his audio recording "The Strangest Secret". So that means that the moment I am taking deliberate action on a goal which I have decided, in that exact moment I have become successful; whether or not I have demonstrated the money in the bank account, or whatever the end result is, is not the issue. The moment I take deliberate action to move me in the direction of my ideal, deliberately, in that moment, I am successful. Certainly, I've had other accomplishments in my life, and because I'm earnest and diligent, I have no doubt in my mind that this is something else that is coming to fruition. So I will now assume the posture of the person who is credible and who is able to perform the actions I am here to perform, to actually generate the wealth or whatever it is I am after. And if you're going to make it in business and in life, you've got to have a great dose of self-belief. This isn't the 1800's anymore; you've got to be on your game. Self-mastery is the greatest game there is because once you get *who you are*, you get everything else too.

DOING

Great - Now that we know who we are, what do we do? And this question is at the root of making right decisions in our life. Let's say your goal is to create wealth in your life, so you're making some business decisions. Well, it's not the person yesterday, who perhaps struggled with money, who we are relying on to make these decisions, to take these great actions in our life. No, it's the person *now*, it's the person we've become now who is called upon to take action. So then the question is, what would *this* person do?

Think in your mind: Now that you're the person who earns the money, has the successful results and all the things that you fully, without any counter-intention, expect in your life, what decisions does that person make? Take it down to every last detail. How do you shake someone's hand? How do you look in the mirror? How do you sound on the phone when you're talking to your prospective client? What decisions does this person make when it comes to capitalizing their business, prioritizing their time, or going to events that could further them in their business or career? Are they diligent? Do they study good information, or do they watch four hours of TV per day like the average American does?

We begin to do things to model *ourselves*, this image of ourselves that we've so totally sold to ourselves through our consistent new way of thinking. And we can build that model through the examples of others. We can build that self-image model by taking character traits from others and creating a culmination of various high achieving personalities, putting bits from this person and bits from that person into our idea of our new beingness, of who we are. And we can model the actions of other high-achieving personalities.

Sometimes when I'm making decisions I ask myself what a highly evolved person would do. Depending on the situation, if it's business I might ask, "What would Donald Trump do?" If it's my relationship with society I would ask, "What would Oprah Winfrey do?" Or in health, "What would Arnold Schwarzenegger do?" Anyone whose results I admire in a certain area of life, I can take that and make it a part of my character. It's almost like building Dr. Frankenstein's monster. There are all these different parts, but the end result is a being that was quite capable of doing various great feats (like crushing things, moaning loudly, causing havoc and scaring people). But you get the point. And this has nothing to do with "fitting in" by the way. Like Frankenstein, this has nothing to do with conforming to the masses. And thank goodness. We wouldn't be in this conversation if the intention was to be just like everybody else and do what everybody else is doing.

HAVING

Having become this new person, and having chosen and acted on decisions that this person makes, I immediately shift the currents of the universe and begin automatically attracting circumstances, the circumstances necessary for the fulfillment of the vision. And this never fails. Those seemingly coincidental circumstances that just show up in the lives of the "lucky" start to show up in my life. I have almost no part in the having. There is nothing to be done in the having of things. It just comes to me. There is no work that has to happen there.

The work was in the being. The work was in choosing the right thoughts. The work was in cultivating the expectation of greatness for myself.

The doing - the activities that I took, my business activities, the decisions that I've made and acted on - that was merely arranging the receiving pipeline. That wasn't the real work. That was the opening of the floodgates. When I placed the advertisements, or picked up the phone, or went to the gym, or made the deal, that wasn't the work; that was the receiving activities. And the having is something that I gave no mind to. There is no effort to be put into having.

So get the equation straight: *The* work is in the being. The receiving is in the doing. The having is not your department. The having is not your area of concern. The universe provides all, handles all the details perfectly, always to deliver unto you exactly what your innermost expectations are. So then the question is, for a lot of people, what is it that you've been expecting? Well, to answer that question, look around. That's exactly what you've been expecting. Again I say *the work is in the being*. If we're diligent in this one thing it will get us off the ground in the direction that we want to go. We must begin using our will to choose the right thoughts consistently enough that we become someone who we weren't before. If we are willing to do that, ultimately, we cannot fail. However, as simple as that sounds, and as simple as that is, the following fact remains:

Thinking is the hardest work there is, which is probably the reason why so few engage in it.
Henry Ford (1863 – 1947)

Here is why most people fail. They do the exact opposite of the BE DO HAVE principle. They live by the "have do be" principle, or lack of principles. They say, "Well, if only I had more money… or better education… or a different location… or spouse… or more luck… or whatever the circumstances are… if only I had better circumstances then I could do the thing. Yes, then I could make those big decisions. Then I could start that business. Then I could make that investment. Then I could take that action. And then, I would be successful. Then I would be this person who I always wanted to be… So if I had the right circumstances, then I could do the thing, and then I'd be successful." Guaranteed failure! And this is exactly what most people do. If we look at our bank account or our appearances in our life and allow that in any way to become our self-image (if we get emotionally involved in *that* to determine who we are being) then our past equals our future. There is no evolution in that way of "thinking".

Here is something that you'll want to make note of and keep in mind as you live from your possibilities instead of your past. There is a great distinction between thinking *of* the end and thinking *from* the end. Most people, when they have a thought about their desires, are thinking "Oh, wouldn't it be great when this happens" or "Wow that would be great *then*." But it's always something apart from them, always something in the distance. It's something that is not a part of their immediate reality. The way of mastery is *thinking from the end*. The inner dialogue goes like this: "So now that I have that result in my life, *now* what am I experiencing? How does *that* feel?"

Sometimes when I'm thinking of a goal I'll think, "Well now that I've already reached that goal, what is my next goal?" And I start thinking of the goal that hasn't even manifested in my life yet up to that point as if it's already in the past. It's like I advanced the video tape, and I'm already planning for my next goal, because after all, once I've hit X goal I'll be on to Y goal. So why not start operating from the place of "Hey, I'm looking to accomplish Y in my life, because I *got* X." This is thinking from the end.

You can see many examples of this in your life just with common things that you do. Think about when you choose to go buy a product. Maybe you saw an advertisement where people got the product, and they are using the product, and then suddenly they are happy and having a great experience. And isn't life wonderful. And you got an image in your mind of what it would be like to be using that product. It would be happy and wonderful. Next thing you know you are buying that product. So the advertiser got you to think from the end, and that thing showed up in your life.

I wanted a new car. So I showed up at the car dealership and I got the brochures and the demo DVD and I took the test drive. And I met the salesman and had the whole experience. I gave myself the experience of driving the car and a memory that I could refer to every time I thought of the car or read the brochure. And guess what showed up in my garage a short while later? This stuff works, whether we know it or like it or not.

And why does it work? I'm one of those people who always likes to know why things work. As a child I was taking things apart and putting them back together to the best of my ability, radios and mechanical devices and whatever. But I discovered in my search for why things work in my life something that has been called the Law of Reversibility. Now listen to this because it's happening right now, and if you want a total boost in self-confidence this could be the ticket.

The Law of Reversibility states that if something is true in nature in one direction, it must also be true in the reverse direction. So for example, let's say that you take two sticks of wood and rub them together. Okay, that's *motion*, right? But what does that produce? That produces *heat*, you guessed right! Okay, great. So then, according to the Law of Reversibility, if motion produces heat the reverse of that must also be true. Heat must produce motion. So where can we find evidence of that? Well let's say we go out to your automobile, and we turn the key in the ignition, and what happens? There is heat. There is a fire that happens inside the combustion chamber of the engine. The heat expands, the expansion pushes the pistons down and the crankshaft turns and the car goes. Therefore, motion produces heat, and heat produces motion. You follow me so far? Good.

So how does this relate to you achieving your goals in life? Well, if reaching your goal (as an example, earning $20,000 per month and sending your kids to private school and buying the new car) produces X emotions (happiness, gratitude, enthusiasm), then by the Law of Reversibility, X emotions must produce that event! It cannot fail! It's impossible.

So how does anyone "fail" in life? Here is how to fail: Look at your current circumstances, your bank account, your credit card statements, your relationships, the reading on the scale when you weigh yourself, and get emotionally involved in *that*. Allow that to determine your emotional state, which reveals who you are being, and you get to have more of that. That's how people fail. What we must do is subordinate appearances to our inner vision. Yes, to have integrity to our inner vision. Vision must come first, appearances and circumstances come second.

Finally, brethren, whatsoever things are true, whatsoever things are honest, whatsoever things are just, whatsoever things are pure, whatsoever things are lovely, whatsoever things are of good report; if there be any virtue, and if there be any praise, think on these things.
Philippians 4:8

The Law of Reversibility is alive in your life, whether you know it or like it or not, but there is one problem with all this. Are you ready? You can't be a victim anymore. Once you know the law, you know that you are in control of your experience. You are empowered to accept responsibility for your results. (Not *take* responsibility, because you've always had it. Now you get to *accept* it!) Do you realize that, in fact, you have never been a victim in your life? That there are no victims, there are only volunteers? And now you get to accept the responsibility, which I think is such a liberating thing.

Psychologists have said that a person's peace of mind is in direct correlation to how much they feel they are in control in their lives, that your peace of mind correlates with how much you feel like you are at cause for your experience. And I would tend to agree with that. But you've got to ask yourself: Do you value success in your life more than you value being a victim? Well, you know what the payoff for success is. The happiness, the love, the health, the money. The feelings of well-being and fulfillment etc. But what's the payoff for being a victim? If you're like many people there has been a payoff there, and it typically comes in the way other people relate to you. If you rely on sympathy or agreement from other people to make you feel validated or important, and if that payoff is more valuable to you than reaching your goals, please give this book to someone else who is willing to come out of the fog and be proactive.

Decide to recognize for yourself right now that your great achievements are within reach, that you are moments away from demonstrating the vision which drives you, and that it is being delivered right on schedule.

When riches begin to come they come so quickly, in such great abundance, that one wonders where they have been hiding during all those lean years.
Napoleon Hill (1883 – 1970)

This is exactly the experience that I had. The missing link between my wanting success and actually achieving success was in my taking the posture of the person who would have it. I began to align my self-image with my perceived ideal and I started to get new ideas. Yes, new ideas came into my mind on ways to further myself in business and in my relationships. And yes, the floodgates opened. Getting congruent with my vision was the missing link.

When my internal dialogue directly matches the image of my wish fulfilled, miraculous results happen.

You'll want to carefully reread that last line a few times. I had to subordinate appearances, which come from my five physical senses, to my inner vision, which comes from the higher faculty of imagination. I used my will to keep my vision in the windshield, and appearances in the rear-view mirror. This was a whole new way of being. And a new way of being induces a new way of acting – behaving, doing. And new activities induce new results - new having. It's just as simple as that.

There is a sure-fire way to know that we are on the right track with our thinking and operating from this position of power. As we said before, it's our emotional state, but more specifically it is the feeling of gratitude. Let's take a look at this. One of my favorite distinctions about the power of gratitude came from the Bible story about Jesus and Lazarus, where Jesus is raising Lazarus from the dead. The thing that struck me about this event was *when* Jesus gave thanks.

Father, I thank thee that thou hast heard me... Lazarus, come forth!
John 11:41 – 43

In other words, the gratitude came first, then the demonstration. Gratitude first, demonstration second. So there was no doubt. There was no "Oh, I hope this works." The operating state was one of gratitude. Of course, Jesus *knew* that he and the Father are one. And in the knowing of that (not in the belief, but in the *knowing* of that) he said, "I thank thee that thou hast heard me" and after that, "Lazarus, come forth!" Here is your demonstration. Beautiful stuff.

So I've got to remember that in my life, this whole idea of gratitude is so essential if I am to demonstrate this great result, this goal, whatever it is that I intend for my life. To have the gratitude first. There is no greater wealth producing emotion than gratitude. Gratitude is the "big cannon". The most powerful wealth creation emotion that I know is gratitude, because it assumes the posture of "it's already done." That it's too late to fail, I've already got it! And living in this state comes with practice. It comes with consistency.

There is no quick fix for this. We're not talking about putting a Band-Aid on a person's mind-set. This is a way of living, and it often requires actions that remind us of who we are. This is a character-building kind of thing to do. For starters, you can make a gratitude list, add to it often, and refer to it when you're feeling negative emotions. As discussed in another chapter, you can re-write your goals, meditate and solidify your vision every day. You can list out and acknowledge every high-integrity action you've succeeded in doing that day. You can give something away, perhaps a small gift or even the wishing of goodwill and success to another. These things assist in assuming the posture of the person who already has the goal. You will see yourself in great detail, having already accomplished your intention, and you will operate more and more from that position, and you'll feel good about it. How does this person do the various activities that you do throughout your day? How do you greet other people? How do you walk down the hall? How do you sound when you speak? How do you occur to other people on this planet when you are this person, knowing that it is already done, that it's too late to fail? You've already got it. Thank you.

"Thank you" becomes your prayer. But I'll say it again, this requires consistency of character. And speaking of consistency and building character, I can tell you that the reason I've become successful isn't because I was already the best at some skill. I'm competent in some areas, I'm ignorant in most. However, I'm consistent. In fact, I'm consistently-consistent with principal-based activities that are important to me. And to the extent that I'm consistent, I develop this self-mastery that we've been talking about.

This is quite a departure from the masses, and of course, so are the results. Take for example people who rely on new years' resolutions to develop some new habit, like new years day is somehow different than any other day. They think "I'm going to have a new year's resolution. Starting on New Year's Day I promise to _____". Notice, they're not thinking "Now I'm going to have resolve", because it's never "I'm *going to* have resolve". You either *have* resolve right now, meaning *now*, or you have no resolve. There is a big difference. The "new year's resolution" is simply a bastardization of self improvement. It doesn't have anything to do with building character or being resolved, because you don't have to wait until New Year's Day to be resolved.

Of what use to make heroic vows of amendment, if the same old law-breaker is to keep them?
Ralph Waldo Emerson (1803 – 1882)

Now that I'm on a rant, let me give you one quick example before I wrap up this chapter: Think about the fitness center, the gym, someplace where I show up at a lot. I go to the gym, I lift weights, I'm in great physical condition, okay fine. And I get to the gym, and let's say it's January, and the gym is packed with new years resolutionists, because what's one of the big things (here in America anyway) that people say they want? They want to lose weight, and they want to make more money.

(Okay, great, yea sure you do.) So they're in the gym. It's January, and by the third week of January or the first week of February the gym is empty again. Now think about that. And the health club owners know this! They sell the memberships, but if everyone fulfilled their memberships, if everyone actually went, there would be a line to get in the place. It would be impossible. The system wouldn't work. But no! They know that people have no integrity! They know the drill: here comes the rush of people, sell them their annual memberships. And they know they're not going to show up.

Consistency! Consistency leads to mastery. This isn't a Band-Aid, part-time effort. This is now. Get off your ass *now*, and *stay* off your ass. Look, there will be lots of time for resting in the coffin. Now it's time for action, consistent action!

-Simple Action-

Make a list of things that you are grateful for in your life. Review it each day, and feel free to add to it or rewrite it.

Make a list of three to five beliefs that you have about life which aren't serving you – things that you don't like, and feel that if they were different you would be more successful. Then write out what the exact opposite of that belief would be. Throw out the list of old beliefs. Keep this list of new beliefs with your goal card and review it often.

Examples:

Old belief: I have no time

New belief: I have plenty of time

Old belief: I can only do so much

New belief: I can accomplish anything

ACTION DOES IT

There is a saying that knowledge is power, and recently I've found some people who disagree with that, and rightly so. Knowledge is knowledge. Knowledge applied (in other words, knowledge plus action) is power. And that could be called wisdom. There is a difference between knowledge and wisdom. Knowledge is passive. Wisdom is dynamic. Wisdom is applied knowledge. Wisdom is knowledge in action. It is the praxis of actually taking a belief or theory or an idea and acting on it. It's the integration of belief and behavior. That's the integrity that I speak of.

Action does it. Yes action. This is the indispensable defining line between whether you're getting the result that you say you want, or if you're someone who sits around and philosophizes all day, wondering why the world isn't recognizing your greatness. And I'll tell you, I've done more than my share of that - sitting around philosophizing about why life is so unfair or why the world doesn't recognize my great talents.

This is so common. How many phenomenally talented musicians, writers and artists go unnoticed? I'm sure you've met people in your life that have seemed to you to be tremendously talented, perhaps more so than "professionals" in their chosen area, and yet they weren't profitable. Perhaps instead of putting to use their gifts or their special talents, they're spending their life working an uninspiring job. But to you, and possibly to them, they've got a great ability which is going unfulfilled. The person responsible for unfulfilled potential is the person who fails to take action in alignment with their purpose. Right action equals profitability.

You can't build a reputation on what you are going to do.
Henry Ford (1863 – 1947)

That's great. And put another way, you don't get paid for what you know; you get paid for what you do with what you know. This is the big distinction. Think about that. How is it that most Americans are struggling financially, and yet we have countless people who have come to America from other countries, who have immigrated here, and who have become very successful in business? They've run the table in their chosen business. Why is that?

Because they're people of action. They're not comfortable and lazy. They put their ass on a plane and got to America and made this the land of opportunity for themselves. I love working with people who have come to this country looking to flex their entrepreneurial muscles. What a pleasure it is to work with those people. They're not trapped in the "society owes me a living" mentality. They're motivated, they're in action, and they succeed. Think about this. The willingness to take action is not something that's exclusive to people who have immigrated to America. If you're an American reading this and you haven't been making your mark, you can choose to get off your ass right now. Consistent action is simply a decision.

This applies to anyone regardless of the position that they are currently in. If you're in a position where you're running a business you certainly have already developed some of this. But even if you're reading this book and just considering the idea of taking a more self-reliant approach in your life, it still applies. You will go to the next level in your life, to the next chapter in your life, once you outgrow this level, once you outgrow your current position.

Look, I used to be a mechanic. In fact, I remember back when I was in school learning how to be a mechanic, one of my instructors gave me this lesson because I had a problem with attendance. This was back in the time when I was always late for everything. And one of my instructors said, "Look, you could be a *great* mechanic, but if I were hiring people I'd rather hire someone who was just a *good* mechanic, but showed up for work every day." The good mechanic gets the paycheck, the guy who shows up every day.

This is a lesson that I still deserve to remind myself of because, yes, I can give 100% of my energy to something and master it, and who couldn't? (If you've got an interest you've automatically got an aptitude. So give it your energy and you'll become great at it, whatever *it* is.) *But,* that doesn't mean that I get to rest on my laurels before, during or after having made great achievements. No! One thing is constant in the universe, and that is change. There is no such thing as a holding pattern in the universe. I'm either moving towards a goal or away from a goal. I'm either expanding or disintegrating, nothing rests. So consistent action does it.

And like we talked about, the time to start is now. I will never be ready. I will never be 100% ready to get started with a new activity, a new discipline, a new approach. I must act in spite of fear, in spite of unknowns and in spite of circumstances that seem uncongenial to my purpose. Especially in the face of circumstances, I must act. There is no substitution for action.

This does not just apply to our professional lives. How about in relationships? I love my wife. My wife is wonderful. What actions do I take to demonstrate that? The feeling of love is not the entirety of marriage. Yes, unconditional love is a great foundation, but the relationship has moving parts in it. What action do I take? I stop and I get the flowers. I go and I get the card with a special message, the reminder of love, affection, affinity, and how I cherish her in my life. This is action. I don't know about most other people but for me (and I assume this is many men) I hadn't been a big flowers and cards type of person. This has been something that I have had to consciously and deliberately choose to do. And the more I do it, the more I get into the habit of doing it.

I am guaranteed a smile every time I open the door for my wife to get into the car. I sometimes look and see people leaving a store or a restaurant and they are going back to their car. How few men opened the door for their wife or girlfriend? Now, if you live in a country where the women open the door for the men, and that's considered a kind and chivalrous thing to do, then okay, fine, do that. But where I come from, an important woman gets her door opened for her. Now, I don't do this every single time, but more often than not, I do. By contrast, most people never do. So get your act together, men. This is such a small price to pay to get such a big impact. At least that's how it's worked out for me. Do your own experiments - cards, flowers, opening of doors. I'm sure you can think of a few other actions that you can take as well. But it's the action that did it. Yes, the silent intention of love is wonderful, but where is your action?

How about when I'm expressing my gratitude to another person for something they've done for me or who they've become for me in my life. I heard someone once say that appreciation is a thought, but gratitude is an action. How about writing that thank you note or card to someone and sending it off in the mail. E-mails are okay, but cards and hand written documents are the real deal. Again, this was not something I had learned growing up. This is something I have to deliberately choose. I take an action to demonstrate my gratitude. Is it enough to be in appreciation and just say thank you? Well, you tell me.

Here is an idea - The Golden Rule. Anybody heard of that? Would you prefer to just hear "Hey, thanks man." or "Here is something that I would like to offer you as an expression of my appreciation."? That could be a gift, a card or whatever. Gratitude is an action, and when you go the extra mile for other people, they go the extra mile for you.

People who deal with me know who they're dealing with. There is no question in their minds about it. They know that I am a person of action. They know that I expect action. They also know that by association with me it brings out the best in them. And by my association with other action-oriented people, it brings out the best in me. What a beautiful thing to be around a bunch of busy people, none of which are interested in buying each other's excuses, or their own excuses. Boy, if we could just get the whole world doing this, transformation would be upon us. It's time to act.

In the past, I spent so much time in preparation. But not really preparation, more like procrastination. What I must do is overcome my own inertia. The amount of talent that is wasted by people who are forever preparing for the ideal circumstances before they take action is unfortunate. This had been a crippling defect of mine for years. I'm happy to say that it's in the past. To quote our buddy Ralph:

Do the thing and you will get the energy to do the thing.
Ralph Waldo Emerson (1803 – 1882)

I am in action! My answer comes when I'm in action. I believe there is a razor's edge difference between successful people and the would-be successful people of this world. Now,

I'm not talking about the derelicts of society who have no motivation to take action of any kind. What I'm talking about are the countless legions of people with so much potential and worthy desires, who never quite get started on the path to their fulfillment. Wishing for a thing has never brought it to me. I have to get off my ass and make it happen. What stops people from getting started in any worthy endeavor? The simple answer is fear. Fear of failure, fear of making a mistake, fear of success (worthiness).

But the biggest and most persistent enemy of productive action is fear of criticism! People don't commit to taking action because they fear criticism. Criticism from their friends, family and neighbors. The driving force behind most people's decision-making is: wanting to look good, and avoiding looking bad. This is a very fear-based way to live.

Seeking approval from ignorant but well-meaning people has crippled more potential greatness than anything I've witnessed. A person has to be thoroughly dissatisfied with their current state of living (results, income, lifestyle) for them to leave the herd. It is the nature of the herd to keep you in the herd. The conversation in the herd is about what other members of the herd think. But that statement probably gives them too much credit. I heard a very learned man once say, "Don't worry about what your neighbors think, they probably don't!"

Why is it that people are so quick to conform? Who cares what the neighbors think!? Does that sound brash? I have never met a high achieving person who followed the masses. I assume that because you're reading this book that you are achieving or seeking above average results in your life. The results of the few, not the results of the masses. Therefore we must abandon approval seeking and become inner-directed people. If people are inspired by our vision and our action, they are welcome to join in the parade. And if not, there is always the sidelines. If, at first we march alone, so be it. Other progressive thinking people will certainly be attracted to us and meet us on the path.

I remember when I was making the decision to leave New Jersey, the area that I grew up in, to come to Arizona. I love the sun. I love palm trees. I like to be warm. I got all sorts of criticism, naysayers assuring me that I would be back. People clinging to their comfort zones, and especially so, because *my actions challenged their comfort zone.*

The first love of my life was music. When I was in a band, I had all kinds of people telling me that we would never put out a CD or draw a crowd. We did both, and gained international popularity in our genre.

When I met my wife, who I've been with for 10 years now, I got all the free advice imaginable from people who had failed at marriage. When I started a business that brings me more income in a month than most Americans earn in three years, people assured me that I was a fool. They're all working jobs.

To avoid criticism do nothing, say nothing, be nothing.
Elbert Green Hubbard (1856 – 1915)

So it seems to me that we've got to put on some armor. My life is so different today than it was years ago. The people in my life are conscious, thinking people and are pleasant to be around. They appreciate other conscious people and are *in action* themselves. My resources are exponentially greater than they were a few years ago. My circumstances have completely changed from what they were. Would I have attracted these relationships and circumstances had I clung to my old way of being that I was indoctrinated into by generations of ignorant but well-meaning people? Of course not. I had to leave one plateau to go to the next. And I can tell you this, I'll never go back. Once you know, you know!

Evolution is an interesting thing. David Hawkins, in his tremendous book "Power vs. Force", talked about the unlikelihood of most people to make any significant progress in this lifetime. In fact, some people de-evolve and have a net loss of progress in this lifetime. But with *motivation*, tremendous gains can happen. Tremendous evolution can happen in this lifetime for a motivated person. I've demonstrated this in my life, up to this point it's been pretty remarkable, and I'm going to continue.

But here's the thing, motivation is lacking for most people. Now why would one person be motivated and another person is not? I've asked myself this from time to time. Why is it that *I'm* hell-bent on success? I was recently looking back on my early life, growing up in poverty and lack, and decided to seek out some people who I knew from my younger days back in New Jersey. I found some of these people on the Internet on various networking websites. I saw some pictures and I saw what they were doing with their lives, and most of them were doing nothing! Some of them had degenerated further.

It was startling, and I started to ask myself, am I the only one who has made it out of the gutter? Why me? Why am I a millionaire, a successful husband, bodybuilder, etc. and these people are right where they were 20 friggin years ago!? Why is it that I am different? How is it that my life works, and most people's don't?

Same thing in business - I currently have a couple of houses in Tucson, Arizona, where real estate growth has been tremendous. And yet, why is it that only a small percentage of the realtors in one of the best housing markets in the United

States of America are earning a profit significant enough to even stay in the business? Why is that? Why is it that few succeed?

Well, obviously some people were motivated. Okay, but why weren't these other people motivated? I started to ponder this. Why me? Why was I motivated, and these other people apparently aren't? If Dr. Hawkins is right and motivation is the key fuel for somebody making big strides in this lifetime, why was I motivated and they weren't?

And the answer is that I believed in myself. I believed in my possibilities, or I believed in my ability to *actually get a result* in my life. I believed that I could, in fact, have a better result in my life. Had I not believed that, I would have never been motivated to take any action. So I had to first have a good dose of self-belief, a belief that my possibilities were real for me in my life and that there was a light at the end of the tunnel.

So how did I develop that belief? (Yes, I'm looking to go deeper into the rabbit hole now.) How I developed that belief is by association with other people who had shown up on my path to demonstrate to me better results than I was getting. I don't know if I consciously or subconsciously did this, but this is what happened. By the example of other people, I became inspired. I became inspired, meaning my spirit was infused with a new belief by other people's examples. And some of these people were great leader type figures in my life. Some of them were unconsciously doing so. And of course, some people were just giving me examples of what *not* to do, which I could easily "rebel" against, and through the contrast of that, I could go in the opposite direction. But I started to make distinctions about success and that it was in fact *possible in my life.*

So the important thing for me was that there were leaders. This opportunity for me to grow in my own self-belief came through the interaction with other people. It came through a relationship with another person. In all of the great breakthroughs in my life, there has been another person as a catalyst. It hasn't been something that I've done alone. And yes, I like to meditate and be in solitude and go to the mountains and all this, and that's a wonderful rest, but my effective reality is happening with my interaction with other people.

So it is of paramount importance, it is a most noble pursuit, that you show up as a success in life. Let's say that you want to be effective at your work, and for whatever your reasons are, you want to assist people in being effective at their jobs. Maybe you're a manager. It is of paramount importance that you demonstrate success to these people. *You are either part of the problem or you are part of the solution* at this point. People will not be inspired by the words you say; they will be inspired by the results that you demonstrate. And all their hopes ride on that. That's how big this is! You are either part of the problem or part of the solution in the lives of these people.

In my life for example, I've dedicated myself to expansion of prosperity-consciousness and the greater fulfillment of human potential. I'm about assisting people in getting better results in their life. So what is it that I must do if I'm going to be of any service to people? I must demonstrate abundance in my life. I play full-out in anything I participate in. I have an easily observable lifestyle that people can see. I let people know that success is real, wealth is real. I let people know that by my example. Look: here's where I was, and here's where I am now. Yea, a picture is worth a thousand words.

So show them. Show people new possibilities. This is what leadership is about. This is leadership by example. Show them the result. And if they have eyes to see, they will see. If they have ears to hear, they will hear.

But leadership is *not* about dragging people across the finish line, or even across the starting line. Leadership is about my own excellence, my own self-reliance. And what is excellence? Excellence is simply *commitment to completion.* That's the best understanding of it that I've ever found. So for me to be part of the solution in the lives of myself and others, I've got to commit myself to accomplishing my intention. I've got to commit myself to being deliberate, consistently deliberate in the actions that I choose which lead to the results that I get.

So the best way for me to fulfill my purpose of expanding prosperity consciousness is to be prosperous. The best way to help the poor is to not be one of them.

So the equation I offer is this:

Success requires action.

Action requires motivation.

Motivation requires belief.

Belief requires evidence. (for me it did)

Now sometimes there are greater minds that required no evidence. We can see this in visionary people who have accomplished great feats for the first time in recorded history. The first climbing of Mount Everest and the first four-minute-mile are examples that are typically offered by people who speak on this subject. These people believe, despite not having evidence. Good for them, and good for everyone else too. How many people have climbed Mount Everest and run four-minute-miles since those first people to do so set the example?

I'm going to increase other people's possibilities for success greatly by providing evidence, because most of us are in our human-ness and very conditioned to living from our five senses, to experiencing reality through our five senses. (And I'm not saying that I'm free from that. Of course, being silent and meditating gives me opportunities to experience a more cosmic reality so that I don't require so much evidence from my five senses to develop belief in myself.) So I'm going to make it a point to demonstrate excellence for other people to see, smell, taste, hear and touch.

Remember, your desire always has the means for its fulfillment right along with it. So if we look for the circumstances that are available to us in our already-existing circle of influence we will find fuel for action.

Which brings me to another idea: There is a big difference between a circle of influence and a circle of concern. Stephen Covey in his tremendous book "Seven Habits of Highly Effective People" discussed this. You'll notice throughout this book that I'm speaking of personal integrity, because that's where it all starts. I've got a lot of things that are in my circle of concern, like what's going on with the American educational system, mass-media, politics, widespread poverty, psychiatry, healthcare, etc., but I know that I will do no good in these areas of concern if I'm not developing myself personally, and expanding my own circle of influence. I operate within my circle of influence. I choose activities that will bear the most fruit in the least amount of time to *personally* get results that will give me the power and ability, whether it is financial or influential, to expand into my circle of concern and start tackling other issues.

Sometimes, people who know that I'm a bit of a rebel send me bits of information via e-mail. (They also know that I don't watch TV.) So they are going to supplement me with world politics issues and things that are going on that they know will get under my skin. Usually I have the sense to not even open the e-mail, but sometimes curiosity gets the better of me. And then I'm off into a rant, a mental rant, and sometimes a verbal rant about what's wrong with this and what's wrong with that. And of course, who am I being now? Now I've become ineffective in my circle of influence, because I'm killing a bunch of time bitching about circumstances that aren't something that I can have an effect with at this moment. Then, for however long it takes until I recover from that, I lose power in my life.

Some people live completely at the effect of what other people think they should be giving their attention to. How do they get anything done? I have no idea. I'm writing this book right now, in a cabin near Sedona Arizona, where I've decided to come just to get this writing done, with no distractions, outside of my familiarity, with no other concerns or urgencies that would take me away from this project. It is very important to me that I complete this, and this is a new experience for me. This is my first book, so I'm actually expanding my circle of influence right now by taking an unfamiliar action based on something that I know I can do and that's on-purpose for me, and then finding the circumstances necessary to fulfill my intention. Damn I feel empowered!

And of course I feel empowered, because my greatest happiness comes from taking on-purpose action, by having integrity to my vision. These actions always involve me in giving something, being of service in some way.

All of my problems have come from *trying to get*. When I shift my focus from "What's in it for me?" to "How can I serve? How can I provide the best service possible? How can I be a part of the solution?", then I get into the flow. The *getting* is an automatic byproduct of my willingness to be of service in the lives of others. This often means being willing to do more than what I am being paid for directly by the person who I am attempting to serve. Think about this. If you're in sales, have you ever given your best service to a customer and only for them to go buy from a different source? But then, haven't you also seen that come back? Somebody unexpectedly came forward and purchased your goods or services, with virtually no effort on your part. Do you think that's a mistake? Do you call that luck? I call that law. It's just how things work.

At the same time, there are no free rides in the universe. If you're a person who only thinks "What's in it for me, what can I get?" you'll undoubtedly find people showing up in your life with the same intention. There are no mistakes. Therefore:

Men do not attract that which they want, but that which they are.

James Allen (1864 – 1912)

So I make it easy for the universe to reward me by consistently being the best John that I can be. This is the price of success. It is consistency and a little discipline. In my opinion, a little discipline doesn't take any more work than living a life of being scattered and tentative and indecisive.

-Simple Action-

Make a list of all important tasks for the day. Number them in order of priority. Begin each day with performing number one. Do not go on to number two until you have completed number one.

Give a hand-written thank you card or letter to someone important in your life expressing your appreciation for who they are or something they've done.

Identify one action that you've been putting off. Do it immediately, today. Once you have completed it, write down how you feel now that you have done so.

SELF MASTERY OR SELF DENIAL

One of the first people who assisted me with this idea of integrity was my uncle George. George is an interesting guy, somebody who I did not know well for the early part of my life (being that he was my father's brother, and my father and I were not able to have much of a relationship when I was a child). I later got to know George a bit better as my relationship with my father developed.

I had an encounter with George at a time in my life when I was chronically late. I would show up late, sometimes terribly late, for appointments and events where I said I would meet people. It was completely disrespectful, now that I look back on it. But of course, this was during a time in my life when I always blamed my circumstances. It was the weather, the car, the traffic, the whatever.

Now, George is an interesting guy. George is not so concerned with what people think of him. He left a career as a big player in a major bank in New York City to do some self-seeking and subsequently wrote his book "What You Think is What You Get" and started a foundation. Anyway, George is one of the people who says it like it is, whether people like it or not. He is one of the personalities that I observed earlier in my life which gave me the understanding that "Hey, it's okay for me to be who I am. I am who I am. Take it or leave it, whatever. It makes no difference."

But in any event, one day George confronted me. I don't remember exactly what I said I was going to do, but bottom line, I didn't do it. And he confronted me with this idea of integrity. He said something like, "Well, you said you were going to do this, and you didn't do this. So how about taking a look at your integrity?" Now, at first I was offended. But of course, George isn't very concerned about offending people. (At least that's my understanding of George.) And when I allowed myself to internalize what was said and stop defending my position (stop wanting to be right) I gained understanding.

This may sound terribly simple to you, and then again it may seem profound, but for me it was an opportunity to get on the path of really examining my integrity.

That simple interaction was a catalyst. That conversation triggered something in me to start to become incredibly punctual in my life and to be very careful with my word. I remember a movie, "The Outlaw Josie Wales", where Clint Eastwood was portraying a rough-rider who was moving to the frontier and looking to share some land with the natives. During one part in the movie, he was saying to the Indian chief that he was not going to ravage their land, and that he would like to live in peace with them. He would respect the nature and the Buffalo, take care of his family, maintain his space, etc.

Now, of course, the Indians did not like the white men, who were invading their land and raising havoc, but they knew that Josie Wales was not one of those blue-coat military guys. He wasn't conforming to their ways of conquest and deception. I remember a line from the Indian chief who was granting him passage and accepting him onto the land. He said, "There is iron in your words..." They made their pact, and Josie and his group were welcome to stay.

I was thinking about that as it relates to my word. Is there iron in my words, or is it some flimsy nonsense? Empty promises, speaking for the sake of hearing myself speak, speaking just to appease those around me and seek their agreement? Interesting question. So thank you, George, for being conscious enough to not require agreement. Thank you for not seeking the approval of someone who was not demonstrating integrity in their life, because I would not have been awakened at that time to a major shortcoming that I was living.

If I don't have my word, I have nothing. When I failed to keep agreements in my life I wasn't just letting others down, I was letting myself down. Can a person speak an intention and then not act on it without accruing self doubt? If I don't believe in myself, what can go right in my life? I have found that when people violate their integrity to themselves, that they also begin to deny themselves actions that would move them forward in life.

Self-denial is a living hell. If I have a talent or ability that I'm suppressing, that I'm allowing to go unexpressed in my life, I am creating my own sorrow through self-denial. If I am allowing myself to spend my days at a job in corporate America when I could be expressing my talents in a way that serves one and all I am not only reducing my potential to earn, I am reducing my own happiness and I am not adding to the happiness of the world. So self-denial doesn't just stay at home. *I am either part of the problem or part of the solution.*

In every work of genius we recognize our own rejected thoughts.
Ralph Waldo Emerson (1803 – 1882)

If I'm not allowing myself to serve others with whatever talents or whatever calling or purpose I feel I have I am punishing myself and I am punishing everyone else. I've got to act. I've got to be willing to go outside of the realm of familiarity and take a risk at being great. And then not only am I personally happier, but I see the results. I see real-time results in my life. Yes, in my bank account, in the quality of my relationships, in my energy levels - my vibrancy.

I've found that my happiest times are times of high integrity *action*. I sleep well at night knowing that I did what I said I was going to do, that I took the actions that I decided to take to move me in the direction of my goals - my vision. That's where my happiness, my greatest happiness, comes from - by being a person of action.

There is nothing metaphysical or esoteric about this on the surface, but it is actually right application of law. Whether or not my goal had come to fruition that day or not is not the determining factor of my happiness. I am fulfilled because I have taken action. I am my own answer. And that answer showed up because I am in action. Yes, I am the answer to my own quest for happiness in my life, and that is independent of the result.

I act in the knowing that I'm going to get the results. And I know I'm going to get excellent results in my life, and I do get excellent results in my life, because I remember that excellence is commitment to completion. I'm committed to completing what I begin. And why am I committed to completing what I begin? Because I know that I am going to get the results. Therefore, I am motivated to take consistent action.

This is a very powerful position to operate from. People seem to be very motivated by gaining so-called "security" in their life. But where does security come from? Where does the sense of being powerful in your life come from? From where does this feeling of confidence come? You may have encountered people in your life (leaders) who consistently display this confidence in their personality. A lot of people think it comes from having already gotten a pleasing result, like you just made a deposit in your bank account. And what an artificial, external bit of false security that is. A lot of people live for their weekly paycheck or their monthly allowances. True security comes from two factors:

1 - Knowing that I am powerful in my use of thought. And, by the way, I always have been. This isn't something that I'm just starting to be powerful with, it's something that I've started to cultivate the understanding of. But the power has always been there. So the first factor in me finding security for myself is recognizing that I am powerful in my use of thought. Look at all these results that I've already manifested! My thinking was at cause. And the second factor for obtaining that feeling of being powerful or secure or confident is:

2 - Knowing that I am willing to take the actions necessary to get the job done. Yes, knowing that I am willing to go to any lengths, that I am committed to the completion of what I say that I want, and that I do what I say I am going to do. For the person who is not willing to pay the price of success there is no hope for security. It becomes a never ending quest of self-denial, which can only end in frustration until one snaps out of it.

How can someone snap out of their slumber and stop seeking security and power from outside of themselves? Typically, it requires a major adversity. Their back is right against the wall. They've proven to themselves so thoroughly that their way of thinking and behaving is not working. Yes, when I can say "My life isn't working in this area", then I'm open, very open, to exploring new possible ways of being. And hopefully you are as well.

With practice, and by becoming a person who takes consistent action and is therefore consistently learning new perspectives - new angles - we don't have to have our backs against the wall before we become open to new possible ways of thought and advancing ourselves. We can become more proactive. So action does it! There is no substitute for consistent, resourceful action.

But of course, action requires decision. Decision requires belief. Belief requires thought.

So the path of self-mastery begins with me taking responsibility for my thoughts. From the thought arises the emotional state. The emotional state reveals who I am being. Who I'm being determines what I do. What I do determines my result - what I have.

And lo, I am in the flow. I find myself consistent at the gym and eating the right foods. I am attracting people into my life who are a reflection of my own high level of self-esteem. Financially, I'm making good decisions. Yes, I'm in the flow, and the flow is a great place to be.

Let's consider a few different variations of the idea of flow - this idea of prosperity - this idea of circumstances and events which are sympathetic with my ideals flowing to me. This could be called "current" or "currency", for what else is money but currency, a certain kind of currency that we use to trade for goods and services. And if we find that we are not in the flow, if currency is stagnating, if we're in a rut and experiencing a time of stagnation in our life, there are a few things that we can do to snap ourselves out of it.

The first thing that we can do is demonstrate our expectation to receive by giving something away. That is an expression of abundance. I know that all my needs are provided for. I know that there is always a door opening, so let me demonstrate that by *being* a contributor. And because in this exact moment I've decided to be that, in this exact moment I make a decision to give something freely, not expecting acknowledgment or return or direct reward. I know my rewards come from the universe. I also know that I can never give anything away; it always comes back. So let me initiate the flow by giving something, anything - a gift, kind words or gestures, voluntary service to a good cause. This brings me to the second idea:

When I'm lacking gratitude and not in the flow (the two seem to go hand in hand) something that I can do to snap myself out of my self-centeredness and my story about how much I lack in my life is to go spend some time with people less fortunate. Spend some time with people who are living in ignorance and can't help themselves at this moment, and be an example to them. Show up in their environment and do some voluntary service. Not only do I gain gratitude for who I am and where I am in my life today, but I also provide an example for others that not everyone is living in a state of desperation. And that could be a catalyst to launch someone into tremendous greatness. I know many of my great breakthroughs have come through association with other people. Can I not give back?

Another thing that I can do if I've identified myself as being in a rut, so to speak, is to stop focusing on *production* and remind myself to focus on *purpose,* remembering that on-purpose action is my answer. If you're working with a group of people as their leader and you want to stimulate some growth in the organization, some increased sales, some empowered people, don't make the common error of creating competition between the people who answer to you. Take the high road and refocus people on their purpose, why they're showing up in this organization in the first place. Remember, purpose puts people on a mission. People don't battle wizards and slay dragons without having a reason to do so. They are after the purpose, the Holy Grail, and with that focus, spontaneous right action can take place. Without that focus we get a lot of forcing; and know that forcing is not current. Forcing does not yield any lasting currency. It is a self-defeating, burn yourself out scenario.

I was thinking about the movie "The Incredibles". Here were some superheroes that stifled their powers in order to be like the masses. What a great story. And look, they grew fat, miserable and broke in the process. That's self-denial! I think about the potential of every person on this planet; it's insanely bizarre that people deny their power, because the all-ness of the universe is omnipotent, omnipresent, and omniscient. So that means that I am in individualization of that all-ness. However, I can walk around in a very convincing state of being a self-induced mental cripple if I'm not aware of that, if I'm not consistently reminding myself of that already existing power that *is*, as *me*.

One of the things that I tell people to do if they want to be more self-determined in their thinking is to stop watching television, stop reading newspapers and listening to FM radio, and to be careful with what they allow into their minds from mass-media. This is something that I've been doing for years and it has accelerated my progress immensely. A lot of people have a challenge with this. Apparently it's an addiction! A lot of people want to defend their position about watching TV, etc.

Now I'm not saying that you shouldn't watch the masters of great sporting events or quality educational programming. I'm talking about the ridiculous drivel that is the majority of mass media programming today. Sitcoms, "shock jocks", vulgarity on FM radio. Some of this is very subtle, and some of it is not. And the worst offender of all is the news. Yes, the news. News for profit and ratings.

I know a gentleman through one of my businesses who worked for a major news broadcasting company in the programming department. He had been doing this for years.

Anyway, one day he went in to work, and there, in one area, were all the news stories that had come in. And in a different area were all the enhanced versions they were going to run. As he was previewing the programming that he had to run that day, he said, "What is this shit that we're feeding America?" He walked out of his job that day, and he is no longer in that field.

It is time right now to stop worshiping our comfort zone, to stop using the vice of conventional wisdom. Often the message is that you are a victim, or that there are circumstances stronger than people. The bottom line is that it's time to act. It is high time for people to start taking responsibility for their results, for their thinking, for their life. And some of this stuff on TV is very subtle, but it all goes back to the idea that you are not responsible for things being the way they are in your life.

How does this show up in our society? I heard someone who is equally as critical about mass media as I am once say that television does not reveal reality, it creates reality. So look around. We have people walking around like zombies. Here we are, in the so-called land of opportunity, if you're in America like myself, and people are walking around resigned to their fate. "Well, this is my lot in life. Well, I'm just a clerk at the store here. Yes, I've been working for years to maintain and survive. But it's not so bad."

Stop letting others think for you. Stop allowing others to tell you what you should think for the sake of agreement. Of what use is it to be able to have conversations that are ultimately meaningless with people who are doing nothing but nodding their heads in agreement? And then you nod your head in agreement, and then everybody gets to agree with everybody, and we get to be on the Slow Boat to Nowhere, all together. Most people don't think! Most of society is just a big group of people following each other nowhere. You've got to be willing to break this cycle. Here is what Wattles said:

> *There is no labor from which most people shrink as they do from that of sustained and consecutive thought. It is the hardest work in the world. This is especially true when truth is contrary to appearances.*
> Wallace D. Wattles (1860 – 1911)

So we can choose to have an urgent approach. If we choose to put agreement with others in front of our intention, our inner desires, our drive, our ideal of who we want to be in our life, we are going to cripple ourselves if we evolve at all, which is unlikely. We will evolve at a pace that may actually result in a net loss in this lifetime. Very few people make big strides in their lifetime. Something that has been revealed, and can be proven scientifically, is that people will never outperform their self image. So I've got to do something bold. I've got to get out of my comfort zone. I've got to abandon some of my most cherished beliefs about how things are, because again, my best thinking only went so far. Albert Einstein said it beautifully:

> *The significant problems we face cannot be solved at the same level of thinking we were at when we created them.*
> Albert Einstein (1879 – 1955)

So if I'm open to having a more resourceful experience, a more happy prosperous wholesome experience in my life, perish the thought that I'm going to do it with the agreement of the masses. I heard someone once say that if a group of people is turning left, and if a couple of people are turning right, follow the couple of people turning right and you'll probably never make another mistake again. This takes courage. Here's another quote:

All great truths begin as blasphemies.
George Bernard Shaw (1856 – 1950)

How many more examples do we have to have before we get bold and take some action? Half- measures avail us nothing. I see no gray area between prosperity and poverty. I see no gray area between choosing health or illness. I see no gray area between living a life by design or living at the effect of precedent and circumstances.

Self-mastery is the greatest game you can play.

-Simple Action-

Take up or revisit one activity, not work related, that excites you. Schedule time for it and do it.

DECISION

This is an excerpt from a letter I sent to a group of aspiring salespeople in my company in an inspired moment:

There is nothing special about myself or any other leader in this company or industry that causes us to be successful. We have simply made decisions that have brought us to where we are, and continue to do so, knowing that we haven't tapped even 10% of our potential. If I'm to move forward in my life (who's life? MY LIFE!) and make my mark, assist my family, realize my dreams, etc. I must do things that continue to raise the bar on my performance, my expectations, my Self-belief. Comfortable? Not always. Reasonable? No. SO WHAT?! How much time do I have here anyway? Do I dare delay my experience and wait for "more congenial circumstances"? Don't hold your breath.

When a person becomes successful an interesting thing happens. They can see the folly of the unsuccessful so clearly, as if they were flying in a helicopter looking down with unobstructed vision at the vast terrain. After years of working with and observing successful and unsuccessful people, and having been both, the biggest folly of all, for most people, is their decision making.

There have been times when I've pondered the magnitude of the bad decision making that so many people demonstrate. It's as if they truly want to fail. The decisions and their subsequent action or inaction appears as if it were a diligent effort to struggle and despair. There are a few reasons for the recurring and costly blunders most people make in this area. Let's take a look at them.

We must first recognize that most people base their decisions on the past. They live in a state of *trying not to fail*. Certainly, we have all experienced pain and loss in life, and it is natural to avoid further pain, but to base our decisions on the past is a self-dooming scenario. What reality is there in the past anyway? And often there is a story about it that far exceeds the actual pain of having missed the mark.

So it becomes clear that most people don't base their decisions on facts. They are simply acting out of reactive programming. They actually don't make choices for themselves. They simply react, like a dog to a stimulus. And they keep getting the same results in their life over and over and over again, and it's a big mystery to them why this happens. They feel like they're victimized by circumstances, but actually, they are just reacting to *filtered stimuli that they themselves are filtering*, so life can be predictable, and they can continue to cope with a reality that's at least familiar to them. So they don't make their decisions based on facts, they simply react to preprogrammed ways of being. Beingness predicated by past experiences. It's a very unconscious way to live. And, of course, this perpetuates failure.

So what is it that one must do? We must be willing to observe! We must be willing to stop thinking that we know so much, and *assume no truths*. That's what we must do. We must be willing to get some distance from our already-known beliefs, and be willing to abandon them if we're going to make any progress. And I know that sounds bold and uncomfortable, but too bad, that's what we've got to do.

I know nothing except the fact of my ignorance.
Socrates (470 BC – 399 BC)

Simply observe. We can hit the "Reset Button" on our mind and stop running the same mental formulas that aren't serving us. It's not actual thinking that we've been doing anyway. It's just running on assumptions based on past conditioning. We must be willing to suspend some of our reactive thinking and simply observe so that we can start making new decisions based on *reality*. Based on facts!

Think about this. Where did you get the beliefs that you base your decisions on anyway? Whose life are you living? Most people have been indoctrinated into a way of thinking that didn't even benefit the people who gave it to them! And it affects the decisions they make in all areas of their life – business, money, relationships, education, government, etc.

Take religion as an extreme example. People have killed each other over this. But it doesn't have to be a holy-war to recognize the narrow-mindedness of people surrounding this subject. There are people who believe that anything that differs from their religion (that they *know is right*) is wrong, or they label it a cult. This is especially so if the members of the so-called cult are living happier lives and getting better results than they are. "It must be the work of some evil cult that's causing them to get the worldly fruits of the devil. But we know better, so we'll suffer in piety, and our rewards come later."

Now, if this sounds familiar to you you've either observed it ten million times, or you're living in it right now, and you're just starting to get the futility, the absurdity, of how you've been living. Your way is right, everybody else's way is wrong, even though you don't even know what the other person's way is. But you would die to be right. And people do. Sometimes it takes a long time. Living in poverty and resentment for decades because our decisions are based on erroneous beliefs is a pretty miserable way to go. We could call it ignorance. Or prejudice. Or stupidity. Take your pick.

This is the way most people live. It's sad, I know. But how else could we explain why the vast majority of people in the 21st century are failing. Clearly, decisions are not being made rationally. Clearly, rational behavior is not the norm. If this bursts your bubble, so be it. You can either be "right" in your previously existing ways and continue getting the results you're getting, or you could be willing to confront reality and stop assuming that you know so much, because you don't. Nor do your social, political and religious leaders. I guarantee you they don't! Assume nothing. Get on with observing, and start to make some decisions based on fact. This is what we can do, this is what we must do, if we intend to make progress. If you intend to get a new result, stop assuming you know so much.

I think about how much intellectualizing I've done and how much time I've spent defending my position on things. How much energy I've wasted doing that. I would debate beliefs that I assumed were true, but had never observed as even slightly beneficial in my life. I am reminded of a profound idea that came out of a conversation I was having with my father and my uncle George some years ago. It empowers me to this day:

No one has ever learned anything by being right.

Because if I'm defending my position on something, if I'm in my rightness about the way things are according to me and my filters, then I am shutting out a whole realm of possibility.

And the amazing thing is that if we really knew something we would have no need to defend our position about it! And that knowing comes from direct experience, direct personal observation.

Those who know do not speak, those who speak do not know.
Lao Tzu

Success isn't complicated. Making progress in our life achievements can be as simple as making a decision to model other successes. The people and organizations that I've learned the most from, the most fruitful things from, are the ones whose knowledge came from actual observation of life, and it showed up in their results. They simply observed how things are, and right conclusions became almost effortless because they became skilled in the art of observation.

Imagine the first caveman to discover that he could roll a rock across the ground. He put some heavy item that he wanted to move on top of it and he was able to move it more easily. Then another caveman saw this and decided to do it also. He discovered that a log would work as well as the rock, and perhaps even better. A cavewoman came along and attached a round rock to a round stick and made an axle. What more distance they could move now. All this from observation, not "reinventing the wheel".

Great news, we've made progress since then as a race. People have accomplished many amazing things since the wheel. Perhaps you've noticed. But if success is as simple as basing our decisions on the observation of other successes, why are so few people succeeding? Simple: they aren't observing success, therefore they don't *know* success, and their decisions are based on avoiding failure and arbitrary beliefs handed down by the people failing in their immediate environment. These beliefs are always poisonous in that they invalidate the self reliance of the individual who receives them. "Don't know what you know…believe us!"

If you're not experiencing the results you want in your life I implore you to stop victimizing yourself and others with the endless onslaught of thoughtless, repetitious reaction that you subject yourself and your society to because it's too much work for you to simply observe, because it would require new thought. It would require *inductive* reasoning about who you are, and it would demand that you consciously entertain a thought about abandoning beliefs which have never served you. This is the work that must be done. Or not. Your choice. People can stay broke and miserable and pathetic and unhealthy until the day they die, and many people do. It's a choice you're going to have to claim for yourself. I suspect since you're reading this that you choose to succeed. If you choose to be blind, I wish you luck (whatever that is).

What are some beliefs that hold people back in indecision? When it comes to money, for example, so often people are stopped in their pursuit of wealth, or in their realizing wealth in their life, by the subtle belief that rich people are bad. Now, they may not come out and say this directly, but people like to be right. People like to be good. Our minds are full of concepts of what's good and what's bad. People want to feel good about themselves. And if somebody (parents, teachers, society, religion, government, media) planted a belief in my mind that rich people are bad… well, I don't want to be bad. So I will find circumstances to fulfill my innermost intention, which is to be good.

So then I'm questioning myself and my motivation, and have all this counter-intention about my desires. What an energy drain. So which belief is right? Are rich people okay? Well, who says what's wrong or right? What does it all mean, except for the meaning that I give it? Let's simply observe the obvious: Rich people are rich. Some are "good". Some are "bad".

Whatever. But if I'm harboring an idea in my mind about the way that I think rich people are, that automatically sets me up to either choose to be them or to be apart from them, and I'll make decisions that will ultimately fulfill that self-image.

In fact, it's not uncommon for people who are living at the effect of their past and other people's beliefs to get offended just by hearing about the success of another who isn't. For example, in the past week while I've been writing this book my business has earned me about $70,000.

Take a look at what you're experiencing right now. If you've got the feeling, a subtle feeling of "oh that rich bastard" or something of that nature, this is going to ruin your chance at becoming successful. We must eradicate the idea that there is anything resourceful about competition in our life - this idea that if you get more, I get less. (A belief most of us got in childhood) We must eradicate competition from our thinking and the emotion of envy from our physiology. No emotion will cause success to run in the other direction as thoroughly as envy.

I recently had some tires put on one of my cars (my Maserati) and I could feel the attitude of "you rich bastard" coming from the worker there who was putting the tires on the car. I gave them their space, I spoke very respectfully, and to the best of my ability I saw that person as a person of great competence and potential. And I guess that paid off because they did a good job. (I see that I'm still overcoming my belief in other people's carelessness.) It came out fine, and then in addition to paying my bill I tipped them $20. And the entire experience changed.

Suddenly they were talkative. I was their buddy. They were eager to give me directions to a place that I was going to next. But I wonder, perhaps if I had not remained conscious during that interaction they could have had more of an adversarial experience. And I could have reinforced their belief in "that rich bastard".

On a side note: I'm thinking that perhaps I've become part of the solution in this person's life because I'm willing to give. I'm willing to share. I'm willing to see them as a person of confidence. I'm willing to give people the benefit of the doubt. Whenever I take the high road it benefits one and all. *Always take the high road!*

So in making decisions, we're talking about putting principles before personalities. Whenever I'm looking for what the next right action for me to do in my life is, I consider which activity is based in principles, which activity is based in what I know for myself and for my life. When it comes to choosing whether or not to begin or continue a specific action, I ask myself two questions. These are questions that successful people ask themselves, either consciously or subconsciously, when making a decision. Two questions, only two.

The first question is: Will this action/decision result in me moving in the direction of my goals/ideals/vision?

And if the answer is yes, the second question is: Will this decision/action cause harm to or diminish the ability or rights of another person/people?

Now, if the answer to the second question is no, successful people take action immediately, without hesitation, without asking a third question. So, again: Will this decision move me in the direction that I want to go? And will this decision hurt other people? If the answer to the first question is yes, and the answer to the second question is no, take action immediately.

If we're earnest with ourselves, this will eliminate a great deal of procrastination in our lives. Now we know what to do. There have been many times when people have shown up in my life, usually in business training scenarios, where they're looking for some direction, and they claim that they don't know what to do. Well again, being self-reliant lends itself to us asking *ourselves* what to do.

But if somebody really believes that they don't know what to do, a funny thing is that if they were asked, "Well, if you did know what to do, what would it be?" they almost always come up with an answer! "Well, if I did know what to do, then I would do this…"

So it's an interesting trick that our conscious mind sometimes plays on us, because if our self-image has been that of a person who is stuck - that I'm a person who doesn't know what to do, or that I have to go slow in my life because other people are, or struggling (in the past) is the reality for me, or whatever - then we're going to have to rip ourselves out of that paradigm. And quite often those paradigm transplants come through the observation of and interaction with others who are succeeding. And if I've been there for people in that capacity, to be a mirror, to reflect to them that they in fact are powerful, then I'm satisfied with that.

People become powerful in their life as a result of making self-determined decisions and backing them up with action. Decision means leaving no escape hatch, burning the boats. In fact, the word decision comes from the Latin décīdere (to cut off). So I cut myself off from any other possible outcome. From the vast universe of possibilities I am cutting off this one possibility. That's the meaning of decision. It's not a whimsical thing.

Give me liberty or give me death!
Patrick Henry (1736 – 1799)

That's a decision. When Hernando Cortez said, "Burn the boats!" that was a decision. Willingness to make a decision, and make your own decisions, could be the one factor that is cutting you off from realizing the results that you say you want, if that's where you are now. And if we're clear about who we are and have developed some intuition, our gut instinct tells us when we're on the right path. I don't even have to look sideways. I'm not interested in other people's opinion about the direction that I'm going in my life. It's a self-reliant way to be. And if you intend to accomplish anything of note, that is the only way to be.

We know it when we've actually done this. There is nothing that will get in our way. There are no circumstances sufficiently strong to stop us. And it's not even hard to do. We do it many times each day, but often for small-purpose, basic survival or instant gratification motives. We decide we are going to eat that day, and we do. We decide we are going to walk down the street and we do. But when it comes to something that requires more vision, that may not offer instant gratification, we can find ourselves experiencing a counter-intention, which instantly leads to indecision – a major enemy.

Napoleon Hill elucidated this so well in his masterpiece "Think and Grow Rich".

Analysis of over 25,000 men and women who had experienced failure disclosed the fact that lack of decision was near the head of the list of the thirty-one major causes of failure.

Procrastination, the opposite of decision, is a common enemy which practically every man must conquer.

And he also said:

Indecision crystallizes in to doubt, the two blend and become fear!
Napoleon Hill (1883 – 1970)

This gets ugly. No intelligent action can come from a fearful mind. If I'm not taking definite action toward a self-determined goal I am inviting disaster.

Here are a couple of examples of what it sounds like if we become conscious of it:

"Well, I don't want to do that (or attempt that) because, what if I try and I fail? And then I'm a failure, and then I look bad to these other people who I like to look good to."

Or:

"If I create these new circumstances in my life then what will happen to who I am now? If I start to do these things, these principle-based activities, and it *actually works* in my life, then I'm going to be this different person. I may not be comfortable being around these other people who I've had in my life, and they may reject me."

And on it goes, until indecision, procrastination, worry, doubt and fear become an accepted norm. Let's snap out of it.

Here is a wonderful affirmation:

I dare to make an ass of myself in front of anyone who cares to look.

Isn't that liberating?

To be able to do that, we must have first *made a decision* on a goal that we are not willing to compromise. We will not suffer counter-intention, indecision and procrastination once the "cutting-off" is established.

As I mentioned before, when we're earnest with ourselves we get clear about the direction we want to go in life. We get a feeling, yes, an actual knowing about what we want and where we're headed. And when we're clear about where we're going we start to attract people and situations to us that give us ideas about how to move forward into the realization of our vision. And in those moments of clarity, we make our decisions.

My favorite reminder about this is the Bible story about the destruction of Sodom and Gomorrah. Here was a place of wicked people to be destroyed by God, but there was one good family living there, and they were told to flee Sodom and run to the hills. They were also instructed to *not look back*.

Escape for thy life; look not behind thee, neither stay thou in all the plain; escape to the mountain, lest thou be consumed... But his wife looked back from behind him, and she became a pillar of salt.
Genesis 19:17 – 26

This is the point! We make decisions in a moment of clarity, with no counter-intention, and then we act on them consistently, without reservation. If we look back we compromise our vision and experience negativity, invalidation and counter-intention. We are stopped in our tracks!

Indecision/procrastination is the enemy. It creeps in through the remembrance and avoidance of past failures, pains and losses. It is assimilated when we leave ourselves open to the beliefs of others, entering into our mind unchecked, for the sake of agreement.

The past is a ghost that cannot hurt you and is not to be feared. But when we give it energy by looking back, talking about it, and commiserating with others about it, we are derailed.

Know who you are, know where you're going and step forward boldly. There is no progress for an individual, save for their own self-determinism as an individual.

Act as if it were impossible to fail.
Dorothea Brande (1893 – 1948)

-Simple Action-

Vacuum Law Exercise: Go into your clothes closet and take out every piece of in-season clothing that you haven't worn in at least six months. Give it all away to the needy. Nature does not tolerate unused spaces. It will fill the void rather quickly with new stuff that you actually like.

WHAT DID YOU SAY?

For anyone who is serious about self-mastery and the deliberate application of the Be Do Have principle, there is a dichotomy which must be addressed: It is the nature of mind - what has been called the *conscious mind* and the *subconscious mind*. Many books have been written about this, and many have argued over the labels, but for our purpose in this book these will suffice. I'd like to keep it simple here.

Your conscious mind is what you think with. You use it to communicate, make decisions, process information, etc. Your subconscious mind, which is often less understood, is your work-horse. It never rests, it operates countless simultaneous functions of the body, it has the ability to locate and deliver whatever the conscious mind demands, and it can even be set up with filters that allow for the passing or stopping of information. This is where your self-image resides. It is vastly more powerful than the conscious mind, as it is not limited by the illusion of a separate ego-identity.

Imagine that your conscious mind is the commander of a vast and powerful army. The army is your subconscious mind. It is a magical army. It is invincible. It can be as big or as small as needed. It has the ability to acquire anything it needs to win the battles it engages in, even if the weapons or tools are in some far off location.

Now, this army lives to serve its commander. All orders from the commander are acted upon immediately and without question. The army does not evaluate commands. The army is so highly trained that it knows how to adapt itself to win any battle, even in ways that the commander does not know. If not for the army's affinity for the commander, the commander wouldn't be one at all.

Now imagine that the commander is in the command center, looking at maps and ordering a great advance. Suddenly, he is distracted by the phone or email, and interrupts his own command with side-bar talk. His assistant walks in and hands him a newspaper that says that battles are hard and the price of weapons is going up. His mother calls next and wants to know if his health is good. A lost bird flies into the command center and starts flapping around his face and drops a turd on his map.

At last, when the commander finally gets focused again on his task, he finds that the army is fighting amongst themselves. Some are advancing half-heartedly; some are arguing that they should wait until the price of weapons comes down. Some are taking down phone lines and others are setting up more phone lines. Some are in line to see the medic because of a sudden headache. Some are dodging low-flying birds.

You may be wondering how the commander gets anything done. He doesn't.

One of the character traits of high-achieving people is their ability to stay focused in present time, and ignore the inevitable distractions that come their way. This allows us to deliver consistent and complete communications between the conscious and subconscious mind. Staying in the "now" and being on-purpose allows us to avoid becoming conflicted in our internal dialogue like the blundering army commander. This is probably something you've observed in yourself in times of great necessity or desire. And, of course, results followed. But why then is it so common for people to be off-purpose, and frantically dealing with distractions that will never bring them satisfaction?

Viktor Frankl wrote a book called "Man's Search for Meaning", which reveals that man is constantly compelled toward finding meaning in life. Having examined my own thinking as it relates to this statement, I have discovered that there is actually no meaning to anything that happens in our life except for the meaning we add to it. Think about this:

A sure way to suffering is to be always living in our story about what something means. Someone may say something that prompts us to start questioning ourselves as to why they said it. "What did they mean by that? Do they not like me?" Something doesn't go the way we expect it should go (a business transaction perhaps) and we could start wondering "Does that mean I am going to fail?" Our child makes a mistake, "Does that mean I have failed as their parent?"

I've had thousands of problems in my life, most of which never actually happened.
Samuel Clemens (Mark Twain) (1835 – 1910)

I can suffer for as long as I choose to add meaning to the drama of my life, and *live in the story that I've created about it.* In the past I took everything so seriously. But with even a little clarity (detachment from my story) I can look and I can ask myself, what does this all mean? Two hundred years from now we're all dust anyway! Why am I taking everything so seriously? What's the big deal? I'm here to have the best life experience that I can, provide the best service that I know how to in my profession, and evolve as a loving being with the other members of the planet. And then that's it. We're off to the next experience. I've got to lighten up. What will it mean 200 years from now?

Now, I'm not talking about discounting my importance as a person or my ability to create effects and be a part of the progress of human evolution on this planet. Among the highest functions that a human is capable of is causing effects in their life. I know that I'm able to create a big impact, because, if not me, then who? I'm talking about the daily minutia, when I didn't get the sale or experienced rejection or whatever. What does it mean? Let's put it in perspective. Adding all this meaning to every little occurrence or activity in life is like driving your car with the parking brake applied. When a person habitually clings to meaning it often becomes a roadblock causing them to subconsciously question if they even deserve to succeed.

Think about this if you've got a story about your own worthiness: Animals don't have the ability to add meaning. Trees and plants don't have the ability to add meaning. Could you imagine a lion who questions whether or not it deserves to make the kill? Of course not. It knows its role. A hesitating lion, one who is not fulfilling its purpose, is soon food for buzzards. And when the lion does make the kill, do the other lions of the pride stand around and question if they deserve to partake of the food? Of course not.

How about the tall tree that stands in the forest with all the little shrubberies? Does the mighty oak have a conversation with itself about whether or not it deserves to be exponentially taller than the other plants with which it shares its forest? No! This is ridiculous. This doesn't even make sense, and yet it's something that humans do to themselves often. We've got to know our role. We've got to know who we are and where we're going. And we've got to be willing to exclude from our consistent internal dialogue thoughts that are contrary to that. Yes, I've got to have integrity to my vision of who I am, rather than living in some story that I made up or that I was sold about life's circumstances.

And this is not an issue of morality and social mores. This is an issue of integrity, of being complete with who we are and completing the actions that go along with that. The auto mechanic who repairs someone's vehicle to specification is in integrity. The elected representative who serves the good of the people is in integrity. The medic who responds to the emergency is in integrity. And, with this understanding, even the drug dealer who stands on the street corner with drugs down his pants is in integrity. And so is the cop who arrests him.

Decide who you are, and then be that.

There can be no question of worthiness. I have a friend who had been frustrated with this idea of worthiness in his life. He was at a point where he was wondering whether or not he deserved to acquire a new car. After all the mental gymnastics and time wasting, and adding all the meaning that he could add to whether or not he should get this new car, he decided "Well, I don't know if I deserve it or not, but I'm just going to get it anyway." And in that statement, he became deserving. He became a person who drives a new car, and now he drives a new car. In the moment of *decision* I become deserving of the fruits of that decision. In the decision to fulfill one's desire is the means for its fulfillment.

Now make this distinction: We've been talking about meaning, not purpose. Everything has a purpose. You've got a purpose or you wouldn't be here on this planet, and hopefully you've identified it as a big purpose. Now look around the room. Look at the nearest door knob. What is the meaning of that door knob? Well, it doesn't have any meaning! But what is the purpose of the door knob? Well, to open the door, and to look decorative and beautiful. Okay, fine. So we are not talking about your life or your life situations as having no purpose. There is a great deal of purpose. We're talking about them having no meaning, which, if you get that, is a very liberating idea. It certainly has been very liberating for me. This allows me to relax, suspend judgment and stop giving energy to the stories that play in my head. And yes, there are stories that play in my head. I am not free of all adverse mind thoughts. I'll have to keep meditating and see where that goes.

One of the first books that I read when I started on this path of self discovery and being deliberate about my life experience was "Handbook to Higher Consciousness" by Ken Keyes Jr. One of the things that I'll always remember that he talked about was that we add suffering to the world just as much when we take offense as when we give offense. Because, after all, I'm a part of the world. Think about that. I'm a part of the world, and if I'm taking offense I'm suffering. Therefore I am adding suffering to the world, because I'm taking offense.

Not just that, whose energy is it that I'm putting into being offended? Whose energy is it that I'm blowing on adding meaning to whatever it is that I'm having a challenge with in my life? Wouldn't I be so much better off channeling that energy into resourceful thinking or correcting the things that I feel are not as I would prefer them to be in my life? But no! I've spent years of my life in thoughtless reaction to life drama. I couldn't possibly quantify how much potentially useful time I've squandered in being right, and in defending my position, and even having a position on some things that were outside of my circle of influence. All wonderful distractions, which make for regular conversation with regular people, but no evolution.

I found the solution to be in taking the posture of a witness - to observe things as they are happening in my life from a detached observer standpoint, and not to be in the John-ness of it all. And to understand, as I do when I'm in a moment of clarity, that everything is the way it is. If I am in a place where I seem upset, this too shall pass. If I'm confident that I'm moving in the direction of my goals, of my dreams, my desires, these circumstances could very well be the circumstances necessary for their fulfillment.

I mean, I've never had all the answers. And great news: *I never had to* have all the answers. But my judgment clouds the reality of the perfection of life. My judgment prevents me from seeing the goodness, the perfection, which is not apparent on the surface. So this is a great recuperation of my energy. This is a great reclamation of energy that I can now use to put into my circle of influence, into things that I *can* do something about, into things that I *can* take action on now.

As I cultivate the posture of an observer or witness, I get to be independent of these mental ramblings that keep most people stuck. These mental ramblings lead to indecision, and indecision has never served me. Indecision leads to doubt. Self-doubt is crippling, because self-doubt renders a state of fear. And if I operate from fear, hope for success is gone. *There is no intelligent action that can come from a fearful mind. And, there is no fear that has come from right thinking.* Absolutely none.

Even in the knowing of this, there have been times when I've succumbed to mental laziness. Yes, when I've been lazy and I've allowed my mind to run riot, and I have to recover from fearful thinking. I look at my goals on my goal card, but it looks like nothing but a lie that I've written down and that I carry around with me to taunt myself.

Here is what I do. I take a step back (a mental pause), and I use an affirmation that has been very effective for me to eliminate doubt in my life. I got this affirmation from Dr. Joseph Murphy in his book "The Power of Your Subconscious Mind". The affirmation goes like this:

By day and by night, I am being prospered in all of my interests.

This affirmation works very nicely for me because of my knowing that *I am*. (My highest truth is that Energy is/God is. All of creation, including myself, is created of that. "God is all there is" is my reality.) I can relax in the knowing that despite any drama or appearances of lack or discord that everything is working exactly the way it is supposed to. My conscious mind has no problem buying that. I remember that *I am not the doer*. I am watching events unfold, that may or may not be what I planned, but I am knowing, yes *knowing*, that I am being prospered in all of my interests. By day and by night, meaning that whether I am engaged in this activity or that activity or sleeping or whatever, the universe is answering my request. So what is there to doubt or fear?

Another thing that I do to overcome doubt is what has been called "embracing the dragon". Think about the big terrible dragons in fantasy movies, and the folly of trying to slay the dragon. The dragon is killing all the knights and warriors and seems invincible. I look at taking the backdoor approach to disarming the dragon, and that is embracing the dragon. So when I'm feeling doubt - and I'm sure that we've all had the gripping fear sensation of the sinking pit in our stomach or the nausea or however it shows up in your body - I notice those feelings, I acknowledge those feelings, and I ask myself, "Well, whose energy is it that created that doubt?" Obviously it's real. I'm feeling it. (Notice that I'm not resisting or in denial about it.) So, then of course I get the answer: It's *my* energy. Therefore, look at how powerful I am! Let me acknowledge that I am so powerful that I created so much doubt that it's making me feel sick! I'm a powerful guy! And in that acknowledgment and affirmation I realize that I'm in control again, and the dragon turns into a gecko.

I know many people are familiar with affirmations, but the majority of people who are attempting to better themselves with affirmations are actually making themselves worse. And the reason for that is they are creating an argument between their conscious and subconscious mind. If I say something that is clearly not true to my conscious mind it is going to reject the idea and I'm going to get a feeling of "You're full of it." But if I choose affirmations, or what I like to call reminders, that do nothing but declare and affirm things that my conscious mind has no argument with, then I'm gaining agreement between my conscious mind and my subconscious mind. Then my subconscious mind is able to do what it needs to do in the universe to bring to pass that which I seek.

The acid test for an affirmation is how it makes me feel when I say it to myself. So if you have found yourself in an argument between your conscious and subconscious mind, and you'll know it because your voice in the back of your mind is saying, "Well, that's not really true", then I would suggest that you start with more general statements like *"Wealth"*. That's it, just the word *wealth*. Or:

Success. or

I acknowledge my ever increasing abundance. or

I am excited about the relationships that I'm attracting into my life. or

I know that my daily exercising is making me ever healthier. or

I am so happy that my body metabolizes everything that I feed it.

Another thing we can do is look for transference between one area of our life and another. For example, if I've been successful in the area of my health and fitness, and I feel the feelings of confidence and accomplishment that come in that area of my life, then I can start to picture the other areas of my life where I would like experience improvement with those same feelings. I can picture experiences in my business life, for example, that would bring the same kind of feelings that I experienced in my physical fitness activities and create new mental pictures and affirmations from that.

One affirmation in particular that I got from my friend Shane came after a discussion about how much work I felt I had to do in one area of my life – overcoming fear-based, erroneous thinking. Now, I had made great strides in other areas of my life, but I felt I had a lot of work to do in this one area, and felt that I was still very much a beginner. And so the affirmation that worked for me was this:

My old programming falls away from my personality easily and effortlessly.

It felt a little weird at first because I was accustomed to working so hard at this, but then I thought "Great, now I don't have so much work to do on myself." I can get on with it. I can stop infusing my activities with the idea that I am lacking, or undeserving, or that I have to go slow.

When I started to make significant progress in the area of wealth creation, one of the affirmations that worked very well for me was just three words:

Wealth Right Now

I said it slowly. I repeated it to myself. I feel the reality of this statement, and my conscious mind doesn't argue with it. This was a breakthrough for me. I was not saying that I want wealth. I was not saying that I have wealth. I'm saying "wealth right now." I'm affirming that wealth is something that exists now, and of course, it does.

I look at the millions of examples of this truth in my daily life. I feed my conscious mind evidence to back up this declaration. I live on a bit of a hill overlooking the city that I live in, and every night there is an abundance of city lights that glow in the valley. I look at the mountains, and there is an abundance of trees. I'm driving in traffic and there is an abundance of cars. Look for yourself! There is evidence of abundance everywhere. There is a wealth of everything. I have no problem believing that.

So wealth is a concept that exists right now. So I'm going to affirm that now. And it feels good. The bottom line is, when an affirmation feels good, I know it's effective. I feel good when I say it. That's how I know if my affirmation is one of quality. I feel that warm feeling like "Yeah, right on!" If I don't get that feeling then it's the wrong affirmation for me. It's not a quality affirmation at that time in my life.

All this inner dialogue leads to our outer dialogue. Our words reflect how we relate to ourselves and our world. So what does our language say about us when we constantly talk about something? I will offer you that *we're in love with it*. Even if it means we're complaining all the time. Guess what we're in love with? In this case, we're in love with the idea of complaining.

Some people love to struggle. Now, they would never admit that, but that's what keeps showing up in their life and their dialogue - struggle. Their internal dialogue and their external dialogue is about struggling. Obviously, they are in love with struggling.

Another way to say this would be that they are *in resonance* with that which they are talking about. That which I give my energy to is something that I am in resonance with. Obviously, I have a direct reality in my life about that which I'm speaking about, so if I'm complaining and I'm being a victim, then what I'm saying is "I love my problem. I want my problem. I accept this problem as my reality in my life."

So what we must do then, and what I have had to do, is be very conscious of my language, to the point where I would stop myself mid-sentence sometimes and say "No. I'm not going to continue with that sentence." I am going to correct that thought right now, and I'm going to give energy to the thing that I want.

You see, being aware of and correcting our language makes a huge difference in our effectiveness. We all have thoughts of fear; we all have thoughts of adversity. An easily noted difference between the masses and the people who are realizing their vision and achieving their goals is that successful people are deliberate about the ideas (words, language) that they give energy to. It's not because they don't have these adverse thoughts or these things that they could be complaining about, it's just that they don't give any energy to the ideas that they don't want in their life.

I had somebody who I felt did me wrong, someone who was rude to me, and I was thoughtlessly talking to another person about the experience that I had and saying, "Can you believe this person? They're so rude...etc." Well, what I was saying at that moment was "That's who I want in my life. I want rudeness in my life. I resonate with rude people. I love rudeness." And the person who I was speaking with was apparently more conscious than me at that moment, because they said, "Don't give it any energy."

Whose energy is it? Whose energy is it that is being wasted right now on creating upset feelings? So, successful people, and I'm talking about outrageously successful people, *don't give any energy* to ideas and circumstances and things that they don't want. They have actually developed a deliberate *ignore-ance* of unfavorable ideas. They've learned to be good at ignoring meaningless distractions, and focusing only on the thoughts they choose.

I see only my objective - the obstacles must give way.
Napoleon Bonaparte (1769 – 1821)

So understand that we can shape our life circumstances by the language we choose. We are powerful in our use of thought, whether we know it or like it or believe it or not, we are. The laws always work. We can say that this is the Law of Attraction or the Law of Vibration, but know that what we're talking about is simply resonance. What we're saying when we're talking is "I am on the same frequency with _____. I am in love with _____. And whatever that is, is what's showing up in my life.

Think of the Internet. You get on your computer and you're browsing the Internet and you decide to go to a certain website. Suddenly you're having the experience of that website on your screen, and possibly on your computer speakers as well. And then you decide that you've had enough of that experience, and you type something else and you go to a different website, and you have a completely different experience. But isn't the truth that all of this stuff was already there? It already exists, but the only experience that you are going to have is the one that you have aligned your receiving device with. You've *tuned into that reality*, so to speak.

Think of a typical am/fm radio. All of the music that you can hear on the radio is wherever you are sitting right now, reading this book. All the music is all around you right now. If you turned on a radio you'd be able to tune into one radio station, and that would be the *only* station that you would be able to experience the reality of. It is the one that you're on the same frequency with. But all of it is here right now. This is what we're talking about when I say that I'm in love with success, or that someone loves to struggle, because that is the operational frequency/vibration. It is the position from which one experiences life.

I remember back when I was a teenager I was very troubled, my life was a mess. I was miserable. I was depressed. I was finding myself. So I sought a counselor, and I was very fortunate to have this great person show up in my life. (Or maybe they just seemed great because I was just so pathetic.) But in any event, I went to see this counselor and I started to tell her about my troubles. And at the first session, this person made a demand on me that if I was going to see her for counseling that I would immediately stop talking negatively about myself. She checked me on my language.

I would speak so down on myself all the time, and she said that was completely unacceptable. Now, of course, I speak excellently about myself, and you can speak excellently about yourself all the time too. Understand that I'm not talking about being braggadocios. I'm actually talking about humility, because what is humility? My favorite definition of humility is *honest self appraisal*. So that means: Yes, I've got shortcomings, I've got challenges, okay. But I also have these great things that are to be acknowledged. In fact, you can't have one without the other, right? It's just the Law of Polarity.

And on the subject of language, we can take this to a very evolved level when we start looking at the language that we use in daily conversation. Again, just like with our visualization exercise, a revealing thing in terms of our reality is the language that we use in the casual conversations we have with other people. So let's take a look at the language that we use in our casual conversations.

Do you use words like *try*? So often I'm talking with people and they're saying, "I'm going to try to do that" or "Yea, we're going to try our best" or "I tried really hard". What a bunch of nonsense. What a disempowering statement. I heard someone once say that to try is to fail with honor. I don't even think there is honor in that. *To try is to fail.*

Have you ever heard someone say (when you invited them to attend an event or something), "I'm going to try to be there"? You know that the translation of that is "Under no circumstances will I possibly be there". And you know this! Do you find yourself using the word try?

Now it's going to take vigilance for you to be conscious of your language on a consistent basis for you to correct this if this is something that you've been doing to yourself, if you've been punishing yourself like this. Here is another one: *need*. Need is probably the most disempowering and misused word in the English language. Think about the word need for a moment. If someone says "I need this", what does that actually say? Well, the first thing it says is that they don't have it, because if they need it, they are without it. So it's affirming lack. And since needs are vital for our survival, that means that if they don't get it they are going to die. And yet, if we take an honest look at our reality we'll quickly recognize that we've always had everything that we've needed, otherwise we wouldn't be here. You wouldn't be reading this book right now. You'd be a corpse. So apparently we've got everything that we need. So what is it that you need? This comes up so often in the area of money. Even if it's just the thought "I need money" it's terribly disempowering. You can take the poverty casserole out of the oven, it's done. Your chances of becoming wealthy with that kind of self-talk are finished.

What about the word *want*? This is a bit more subtle, but often it is used in a way that affirms lack. Keep in mind that you can never have anything that you want, because if you're wanting it, that means that you don't have it. And so often people engage in self-talk or conversations with other people about wanting this or wanting that. And what they're saying is that this thing is apart from me, it is not a part of my experience.

Even in prayer, people sometimes tell God what they want, and they place their order, and what does the Scripture say… Ask and ye shall receive. And then they wonder why they're not getting what it is they asked for. But they *are* getting what they asked for! They said, "I want _____." "I want the ideal relationship in my life." "I want wealth." "I want a healing." Etc. And so their prayer is answered - they get to *want* these things, and sure enough, it's delivered perfectly, in real time, in common hours, their wanting is fulfilled. Brilliant!

These are just a few examples. So take a look at your language and see if it's worthy of you, the greatness that you already are. This will pay you huge dividends for as long as you live.

One more thing we can do as we are examining our language is to simply reframe the statement that we make to a different time. In other words, instead of affirming "I am always late" we can catch ourselves and say "I have been late" or "I have had a history of lateness." The idea is to never bring that error into our present reality. The challenge may have been just five minutes ago, but it's still *not now*. Let's not make assumptions that the future is going to equal the past, otherwise we doom ourselves. Keeping the past in the past opens up a world of possibilities.

If someone calls me to brainstorm about some issue that they are having a challenge with and they open the conversation with something like "I'm struggling with _____" I'll immediately correct them in their language. I'll ask them to "Please affirm that you have struggled with _____. And I believe that the purpose of your call is that you intend that the past does not equal the future. So therefore, let's not affirm that you're struggling, because if that's the case, I can't help you. I can't be of any benefit to you right now, because you love to struggle."

Simply shifting time in our speech creates a whole new reality for our self-image. And make no mistake about it - it *is* that vital that we do this. If we continue to perpetuate language in our lives that leads to a self-image based on who we were yesterday then we've got no possibilities. You can never outperform your self-image, it's absolutely impossible to do so. Regardless of how hard you may work, it is actually your self image, your subconscious mind, which makes your choice of success or failure. Think about this. Here is an example:

You're in an airplane, and you're taking off from whatever city you live in and you're heading to New York. (If you live in New York just pick a different city) The plane takes off and the pilot activates a mechanism called the *autopilot* in the plane. The autopilot is a system that has the ability to be programmed to a specific destination, measure any deviation from that course and make any corrections necessary to ensure the correct destination. It works the same way as our self-image. So let's say that midway through the flight you somehow find yourself in the cockpit of this plane and you decide that the plane should go to Miami instead of New York, so you grab the wheel of this plane (I don't know if there is actually a "wheel" in the plane, but whatever) you grab the wheel, and you start steering the plane towards Miami instead of New York.

Now, what happens? There is a lot of resistance. You're fighting against a pre-programmed system that's designed to make whatever corrections are necessary to get this plane to New York. You make one adjustment, and the autopilot makes a counter-adjustment. And you may work really hard and momentarily force that plane in a direction off its predetermined course, but what would happen the moment you let go of the wheel? The autopilot would take over and the plane would continue exactly on its course to New York.

So you see, force doesn't work. If we're looking to change our course in life, the easiest and surest way to do it is to change our self-image. When our conscious and subconscious mind is in alignment, we are spectacles of effectiveness. Use every possible strategy to put the Be Do Have principle into effect immediately in your life, and dazzle the spectators with the results that you get in an amazingly short period of time.

-Simple Action-

Integrity-can Exercise: Keep a metal can or similar receptacle that can hold money in a specific location in your house. Whenever you catch yourself using disempowering language put a dollar in the can. The whole family can play, and it can be fun, but no arguments about policing each other. People have to hold themselves to account. At the end of the month, give the contents of the can to some worthy cause.

The stakes are raised when you're not at home. When you're in casual conversation with others in society, if you find yourself using disempowering language, take a bill out of one pocket and put it in the other. It could be a $1, or if you're out of $1's it could be a $5, or a $20 or a $100! Put the money in the can when you get home.

Create or adopt one affirmation that you feel great about. It should make you feel strong and empowered every time you think or say the words. Write it down and keep it with your goal card. Post reminders of it in your workplace and other living areas. Keep it simple. When you think of another one, do it again.

WHERE ARE YOU GOING?

Throughout this book I have made comments that would infer that all worldly success is spiritual, and that there is nowhere in my life that spirituality isn't. I'm sure you've noticed that I've made reference to several bigger-than-John ideas. What I'd like to do now is show you under the hood and take a more detailed look at my understanding of the engine that runs this success machine that I walk around in.

While I believe that spiritual understanding requires spiritual discernment, the only way I know how to communicate with you here is with words and a brain. So let's not belabor too much intellectualism. The words are not the truth, they merely point to the truth.

And on that note, let's clear up any added meaning that we may have about words that have accumulated a lot of baggage over time. Words like *God*. I feel that many people are walking around with limiting and erroneous meaning attached to their concept of God, and this is so unnecessary. This is of course the fruits of ignorance, perpetuated by the hypocrisy in much of modern organized religion, in the name of controlling the herd. This has nothing to do with spiritual discernment.

When I speak of God, I am simply referring to the power which animates all. It has been called Energy. It has been called the Self, or true Self, or higher Self. It has been referred to as Universal Power, First Cause, the I Am, Pure Potentiality, Shiva, Brahman, etc. This is the power from which all things are created. It is infinite stillness, from which comes all dynamism. It is the inexhaustible source, which supplies all realities. Perhaps you would like to add some of your own words to this potentially endless list. Feel free to do so if that makes you feel like it's complete and you can move on. The bottom line is: It is the Truth which is prior to my thoughts about it. Words about it only limit *us*, since it is not something that can be limited. So, since I like the word God, and because it's easy to spell, I'm going to use it.

Earlier, we talked about the idea of our personal worthiness of success. Often I find people who are conflicted in their intentions about success, because on one hand they want results, but on the other hand they harbor erroneous ideas about it. Many people have a subtle (or apparent) belief that there is virtue in poverty. Many people believe that if they get more out of life that others will get less.

Have you ever heard someone say, "If it's God's will for me then I'll have _____." "God-willing, I'll lose the weight." "God-willing, I'll meet the right person." "God-willing, I'll get the money." I hear confusion when I hear things like that. God was always willing. How about: You-willing.

More extreme is the evangelical type, or the "transformation junkies", with an abundance of devotional sayings about their "faith". But for some reason, that person is never an action-taker.

There are many people who think that God is somehow this strange phenomenon outside of them that's going to do something *for* them. And yet I've heard it many times, perhaps you have too, that God can only do for you what God is doing through you.

So on one hand; I am not the actual provider of the results in my life. I am not the doer. On the other hand; God helps those who help themselves. God doesn't steer a parked car. So when people say something like, "This is what I really want. But if it's God's will for me…" I know they are headed to Excuseland.

Ask, and it shall be given you; seek, and ye shall find; knock, and it shall be opened unto you:
Matthew 7:7

Here's the question: How do you ask? It is by the Law of Vibration that the communication is made from the mind of man to the infinite correlating Power. This is actually what we've been talking about throughout this book. Vibration, frequency, emotion, beingness - this is the language of the universe.

What things soever ye desire, when ye pray, believe that ye receive them, and ye shall have them.
Mark 11:24

Look, some people love to play sports. Some people love to be rock climbers or salespeople or artists or doctors or whatever. Now, not everyone has the same desires, do they? So apparently you've got a desire or a quality of desire that is unique to you. Why question it? Like we said before, when successful people make decisions they ask themselves two questions: Will this decision move me in the direction of my goal? And if the answer is yes: Will this decision violate the rights of other people. And if the answer is no, there is no third question, they take action immediately. Nowhere in that internal dialogue was the question: Is it God's will for me?

Here's the reality: I've got this desire because that *is* God's will for me, whatever that desire happens to be. Otherwise I would not have had that desire. I don't believe that God expresses a desire in people without also providing the means for its fulfillment. In other words, the purpose of life is *to have the experience.* The intention of life is always towards greater experience, or greater expression and expansion. The purpose of life as I see it is for God to experience God through different aspects of its own attention to Itself, individualized, in this case, as you or as me. That's it. So, since the purpose of life is to have the experience, the desire that we have for whatever experience we want is God's will for us. This way, God can experience *that* through us, individualized as us. So let's never question what God's will for us is. It's a silly question. We've missed the point. It's always about expansion and fuller expression. So if you're fulfilling your desires, you're living on-purpose.

Consider this example. Suppose I gave you an opportunity to go to Las Vegas. Not that everybody would like to go there, but this is a pretty clear example for people to understand, and Vegas does have lots of entertainment and shows and things to experience. And let's say I gave you a blank checkbook and said, "Okay great, go to Vegas and live it up." See the shows, play the games, the slot machines, the cards, the gambling, whatever. Ride the simulators, the attractions. What's that thing that's popular now - the Segway personal transport things? Do that too if you want. Live it up. See the crazy acrobatics, and gamble on the tables if that's what you like to do. Etc.

Now here's the catch - when you're done, when you come back, if you win money while you're there, you've got to give me the winnings. So I'll take the money back. Now if you lose, okay that's no problem, give me back whatever checks are left in the checkbook and don't worry about it. Just go have a great time.

Now isn't this what life is? You come to this place. You have an experience. You play the games, you see the shows, you entertain yourself. Hopefully, you do some resourceful things as well and contribute to the experience of others. Maybe you master some games and hit the jackpot, maybe you don't. You don't keep any of it. When you're done you're done, and that's it. So now is the time to have the experience. I believe that's why we're here, for God to experience Itself through different aspects of its own attention to Itself, in this case… you. So you can't lose.

Therefore, I believe that God is all there is. Or, like the quantum physicist, we could say: everything is energy. A lot of people say "God is everywhere", except their behavior doesn't actually reflect this. They don't *really* believe that. There are a lot of people walking around claiming to be devoted to whatever eastern or western organized religion they find themselves in or they've been indoctrinated into, and yet their behavior would indicate that they don't believe a word of this stuff.

The boldest personality of all was Jesus when he said:

…ye shall know that I am in my Father, and ye in me, and I in you.
John 14:20

That was a statement of oneness. That was a statement of humility! (Honest self appraisal) And He didn't just believe it, He *knew* it.

So think about that. What an egotistical, separatist and self-condemning position to take, to think that God is everywhere except right here, except with me, except *as* me. What a non-humble position to be in. When we take these beliefs and we actually integrate them with our behavior magic happens in our life. No lip-service here. We've got to stop paying lip-service to the truth. And some of the people who have the most to say about their "faith" have the worst results.

Therefore, I don't waste my time and my breath debating Scripture. I know that God is all there is. All of creation, including myself, is created of that. And this truth is independent of whatever words I may say about it. Knowing this, tremendous power and possibilities open up in my life. Suddenly, the following statement makes sense:

> *...the works that I do shall he do also; and greater works than these shall he do...*
>
> John 14:12

So people actually condemn themselves to various levels of mediocrity by insisting on a separation between them and the Source. And, of course, this is part of the game of life – the human condition. If not for the illusion of separateness, how could we have an experience of being, doing and having? Once we've arrived in the realization of "I am That", no more game.

On a worldly level, many people do the same thing; they create a separation between them and the successful person, between them and the guru, between them and the master. And as long as you're a subordinate of the master, you get to be that. But if we actually internalize and embody the words that have been given to us by the great masters we immediately gain tremendous power and possibility in our life.

Throughout this writing I've referred to mostly Christian teachings because I grew up in the west, but we could find parallels throughout any culture. We can refer to the Bhagavad-Gita, the Koran, the Torah, the Zen and Buddhist teachings, etc. There is only one cause, and that cause is *at cause* for the effect which we are experiencing as this incarnation, this life experience. As above, so below. As within, so without. The microcosm and the macrocosm. The word becomes the flesh. The yin and the yang. Shiva and Shakti. The wave and the particle. On earth as it is in heaven. And on and on it goes.

And when I actually integrate my behavior with that belief-set, magic happens in my life. I am free from having to be the person with all the answers. I am free from having to know how everything is going to work out. And I acknowledge that things work out, that "the planets align" and that everything comes together right on schedule. There is an infinite correlating factor at work here. I am the beneficiary of all the information, all the knowledge and all the wisdom that ever was, is, or will be because I am an individualization of that.

I remember back in the 1980s, a song that was popular on the radio had some lyrics in it that went like this: "God is watch-ing - us — from a distance." What a bunch of crap! A big hit though, since people are already convinced that they are separate from the all-ness that is their true Self. It's very romantic. And we can give up all of our responsibility for our results, we can give up all of our co-creative power, we can give up all our willingness to have an awesome experience on this planet for the deferred paradise that will be bequeathed unto us by this strange phenomenon outside of us after our death, after our experience on this planet has ended. Very romantic. It's okay that I suffer now because my reward comes later. This is *lack* thinking. This goes hand-in-hand with poverty consciousness. This is an excuse for not getting anywhere in your life. This is an identity crisis on a spiritual level.

Do I understand anything that the Master said? Well, if so, it will show up in my experience. When? Now. Not some deferred better reality that comes after this reality. As far as the afterlife, I can't speak intelligently about that (perhaps in my next book), nor do I see it as having any bearing on how I live this John experience that I'm having right now. I need not be motivated by threats of damnation in order to take high-integrity action; I take them anyway. I know that I've been given a great opportunity *right now*. I've got more ability and resources than I can possibly use in this lifetime. It's my responsibility to develop and experience as much of that as I can in this lifetime. What a waste to go through life deferring the experience.

The Buddhists say that we've had countless incarnations; that we've taken all kinds of forms, from animals to kings and queens to peasants to earthworms and insects to you name it, and to have a human experience is a very precious and rare experience. So to squander or to put off or to avoid developing ourselves is just a terrible waste. Urgency is upon us. We have an opportunity to develop our consciousness while we have this rare and precious human incarnation.

And speaking of Buddhists, Buddha apparently didn't have any problem with identifying with the all-ness that he is. When asked, "Who are you?" His response was "I am awake." Another bold statement from somebody who actually gets it! Now if I could only *get it* on a consistent basis. There's an interesting idea. How effective would that guy be on the planet?

I was at a golf tournament in Arizona, a fund raiser that was hosted by one of the companies that I work with. At the end of the function there was a luncheon. A group of people were gathering and being social and having lunch, and naturally the topic of discussion went to business, because it was a business group and business people like to talk about business. I remember sitting at one of the tables inside the tent (shade is a popular thing in Arizona) and as the crowd of people grew, various conversations were happening. A few people were asking me about some of my marketing strategies, asking me about the "how to" of my business and how I'm getting the results I'm getting. We talked for a bit, and I got to the point where I stopped and said, "You know what? The thing that has made me more money than anything is…" (at that moment, a silence came over the group) and I said, "…daily meditation."

I just stop. Stop thinking. I get out of my head, release my mind-thoughts and get quiet. And I commingle that practice with my income producing activities. That has made me more money than anything. Now perhaps you can relate to a time when you felt really clear, at peace, present, in the now, and the phone rings, and you've got a very fortunate occurrence, a piece of good news, or a sale came in, and you had almost nothing to do with it. This was not something that was laborious for you. This is the experience that I'm talking about. I have this experience often. This is not an uncommon thing when I'm consistent in my meditation.

You can call it meditation. You can call it being quiet. You can call it being in the gap between thoughts, or connecting with the Source. Call it whatever you want. What I find is that meditation is an opportunity for me to operate at a higher level than John. The thing that happens for me when I am in my meditation is that I am actually sidestepping my reactive mind, sidestepping all my reasonable-ness and John's best thinking. I'm allowing myself to be connected with the essence of who I am - the essence of how everything works, the field of pure potentiality, as it has been called. I'm allowing myself to connect with that, and that imbues my activities with the qualities of the field of all possibility.

So apparently, I am not the doer! And what a stress reliever that is.

Yes, I took the action. Yes, I made preparations. Yes, I did the income producing activities that I knew to do to run my business. But the details were handled by the universe, the infinite correlating power.

I'm thinking of a story I heard about a time when a group of people were trekking through the desert and were desperate for water. They went to their leader (Possibly Moses? I'm not sure.), and said that they needed water, and he tells them to go pray for rain. After a while, however long it was, they come back and say something like, "Oh, God has forsaken us! It has not rained." So the leader went to look around, and he said, "Where are the ditches?" And they said, "What do you mean?" He said, "Well, if you expected it to rain, if you expected your prayer to be answered, you would have dug the ditches. You would have made preparations to collect the rainwater. Where are the ditches?"

So yes, I dig ditches in my life. But I'm not at the point yet where I can control when the rain clouds are rolling in and from which direction they come. Fortunately, that's not something that is necessary for me to control in order for me to have the experience that I choose to have in my life.

You know, so many people believe that success is complicated and that they have to know every bit of minutia before they take action. Now I am not discounting the fact that that there is always a need for knowledge, especially if you're going to be an innovator in business. What I'm saying is that my greatest strides, my greatest results, have come in times when I clearly recognized that I was not the doer.

Here is what has been called: the Law of Least Effort. Deepak Chopra wrote about this in his book "The Seven Spiritual Laws of Success", where ultimately, and I am not there yet, but ultimately, we do nothing and accomplish everything. So that being said, this is something that requires some faith on my part, because I have been such a hands-on person. A person who has to know why everything works, and why things are the way they are, and so damn intellectual. I can run that game on myself forever if I choose, or I can do what it says here:

...seek ye first the kingdom of God, and his righteousness; and all these things shall be added unto you.
Matthew 6:33

In other words, my integrity to those words has to be there for me to experience the benefits of that teaching, that I am not the doer. And I can see many times where I've attempted to force solutions on problems, only to create new problems. So this is a very liberating thing when I can get to that place. And being quiet has been the thing that has brought that to me.

So the *work* is in the being. Let's revisit the Be Do Have principle. The work is in the being, in the becoming. It's in the use of thought, in the choosing of the thought consistently enough that I become emotionally involved in the thought. And how do I know who I'm being? I can ask myself one question, and *who I'm being* is revealed. The question is: "How do I feel?"

Well, if I've been thinking the right thoughts consistently enough, naturally that's going to lead to an emotional state. So if I am happy and relaxed and feeling confident and enthusiastic, then that's who I'm being. I'm being that. If I'm stressed out, anxious, upset, resentful, etc., then that's who I'm being. So the work is in the being.

And then I take the action. I go to the gym and exercise. I'm present in my communication with others. I do the income-producing activities that I do in my business. But that's not really the work. That's the receiving. The actions that I take are the receiving part. The work is in choosing the right thoughts, getting emotionally involved with those thoughts to the point where that's what I've become. And since I'm operating *from* that position, I am now attracting circumstances that correlate with *that*. And then I go through the motions to do what I've decided to do in my life, and the receiving takes place. But the work was in the being. That is THE work.

I would like for you to think of a slide projector. I remember way back in the 20th century, back in the 1970s when cavemen walked the earth and pterodactyls flew overhead, people had slide projectors. Do you remember these? There was a rotary carousel on top where people could load a seemingly endless quantity of photographic slides (film) and subject their friends and family to hours of viewing on the big screen, complete with live narration, all in the comfort of their home. "Here are the baby pictures. Oh look… more baby pictures." Perhaps you have had this experience.

I'd like for you to consider that the slide projector has a light bulb inside of it that emits pure white light through a lens that is aimed at the screen, and that the screen is a pure white screen that will render the image. Now consider that we have different kinds of slides, different images that are going to be positioned in front of the bulb and projected through the lens and onto the screen. If I'm looking at the screen and I don't like the image that's being projected, all I have to do is change the slide, the filter through which the pure white light is going.

The white light is pure. The bulb can produce any image on any slide that I put in front of it. It's not limited. In fact, it has no preference about what slide, or filter, the light is going to pass through. The bulb is the source. It's just being the bulb. The screen has no preference either. Without a slide the screen is showing the reality of pure white light. It's showing the potential for whatever visual experience I'd like to have. Now if

I'd like to change the experience, all I've got to do is change the filter through which the light is shining.

This is not a complicated concept. This is something very simple that we can all understand. You get to experience any image (reality) based on the filter through which the light is shining. If we would like to change our experience, all we have to do is change our filter. And self mastery is about being deliberate in our choice of filters.

It has been said many times that reality is subjective. Reality is not *as it is*, but *as we are*. I am always my own experience. My experience of this life, this incarnation, this planet, this human experience that I'm having at this moment is subjective to my filters. So what more noble of a game could there be than self mastery?

In studying how the mind works and how I get the result that I get, I've learned of a few universal laws. One of which is the Law of Perpetual Transmutation of Radiant Energy, which basically says that *energy is*, and is constantly moving into form, and through form, and transforming from this form into that form, etc. But all the energy that is, already is. And we are just going to "create" with it (demonstrate) whatever we are going to create.

So knowing that, if I'm looking to, let's say, demonstrate abundance in my life - I'd like to have increased income, lifestyle, etc. - the degree to which I experience the abundance, the wealth, is to the degree that I have developed my consciousness of wealth. Yes, prosperity consciousness is a state of mind. And because that's who I've become - a person who habitually thinks wealth - this is what shows up in my life. I didn't always like the pictures that were put up on the slide projector. Well now it's nice to know that I have control, that I have the ability to choose the slides. So goes the Law of Perpetual Transmutation.

So the bottom line is: The truth is prior to my thoughts about it. Since I'm in control of the slide projector, I can say with full integrity that I am always at cause for my own experience. In fact, the slide projector has no knowledge of whether or not you're enjoying the experience. I heard Dr. Tom Johnson once say, "God has never been aware of your problem…because all It knows is Itself." Fullness, completeness, wholeness. Right now, all of it, right here right now. The bulb and screen could be the truth. The film could be my thoughts. The truth is prior to my thoughts about it.

But then the question is: What do I know anyway?

-Simple Action-

Sit and meditate for at least one half hour per day. The idea is to get to a place of no-thought. You may focus on your breath, or any other point of concentration that warrants no evaluation in your mind.

Once you have done this, visualize your intention in great detail. Feel its reality, and the emotional state of having realized your intention.

Then write the details of your vision. You could possibly rewrite your vision or goals every day as the image crystallizes and becomes more specific.

OPPORTUNITY KNOCKS

Man is not the creature of circumstances, circumstances are the creatures of men. We are free agents, and man is more powerful than matter.

Benjamin Disraeli (1804 – 1881)

It was a blazing hot 110°F on that June day. I was heading into work, again, where I typically spent 80 hours per week behind my desk providing the best service that I knew how to provide at my job. I walked into my office, and instead of finding what I would typically find there, I found that my office had been broken up into cubicles and my desk was shoved in the corner. There were people there who I certainly did not expect to be in the space where I operated. I was confused. Naturally, I went up to the boss's office to find out what was going on. I had received my third pay cut for the year. The company, however, called it a promotion. Apparently, the agenda in corporate America is not to empower people, but to keep them under control.

I had recently gotten married, just a couple months prior, and I was living at the top of my means. I was barely paying the mortgage on time. The stress had started to catch up with me. Having been a hard charging, overachieving type personality all of my life that I can remember, I was willing to put in the hours. On the one day per week that I did have off from my job I would fall asleep on the couch, to the dismay of my new wife. I had no energy left to even enjoy my day off. I had lost track of how long I had been living like this.

One day I was so weak that I was unable to move from the couch. My wife insisted that I go to the hospital. According to the doctors there, I had developed a stress induced colon infection. I was so dehydrated that I passed out when they drew a little blood for testing. They informed her that this would kill me if I continued in this way, but I didn't know what else to do.

I recovered from that incident, and a short time later there was an opportunity for my wife to visit some family back in New Jersey. She went away for the weekend, and I locked myself in the house for two days, just meditating and contemplating on "How did I attract this adversity into my life?" Now, my goal at the time was to earn $20,000 per month. I thought, "Boy, if I could just earn $20,000 per month... I've arrived!" And for years that had been my goal.

I had been down the road of franchising, investing over $100,000 and 90 hours per week. I did multilevel marketing for 2 1/2 years. Now I was in the car business, all the while never reaching that goal. Every time I got a little bit closer, or every time I got a little too powerful at my job, they would find a way to "promote" me. And of course, "Congratulations John, here is your new pay plan. Sign here." So I stayed in the confines of my house for two days and I contemplated this adversity that had come into my life yet again.

Two days later, I emerged from my house with an understanding that one door closes and another opens. Certainly we've heard that many times. Well, let me add something to that: One door closes, another opens, but it's dark in the hallway.

I seldom know where my "great good" is coming from. What channels, what combinations? What events might take place for the fulfillment of my ideal, of my dream? So what I have to do when I'm in that dark hallway is I have to understand that adversity is only an *investment in my imminent and inevitable success.* No longer looking at adversity as a problem, but looking at it as an opportunity. The door opens, and I'm able to see through that dark hallway to the little bit of light coming through the door that has just been unlocked.

So anyway, two days later I emerged from my house, and I had discovered an advertisement that somehow showed up in my life. I wasn't necessarily looking for this. The ad spoke of an opportunity to earn about $20,000 per month. And I thought skeptically, "Yeah right." But hey, I've got an open mind, so I'm going to do my due diligence. I'm going to find out.

It was for real.

I got started, and within 90 days I had reached my goal. Now, had I not received that pay cut I may still be working that job. I may be dead by now, I don't know. I don't have a crystal ball. Here's what I do know: That when we have adversity, it's an indicator. What adversity is saying to me is that I'm really close to my goal. I'm really close to that next plateau. I am detaching myself so thoroughly from the plateau that I'm currently living on, that I'm currently operating from, and I'm no longer in resonance with that. That's no longer working in my life, and now I'm getting to this next plateau. So it's an indicator that I'm getting very close to my goal.

Don't marry the vehicle! That was exactly what I had asked for, and the universe was responding. I had outgrown my place there. I was going to $20,000 per month. That's where I was going, but not in that vehicle. So don't marry the methods. Decide what you want, know that you'll receive it, and don't expect to have all the answers about how it is going to happen.

If we want to, we could also look at adversity as an opportunity to prove ourselves to the universe - that we are worthy and ready to go to the next level in our life. Hey, I'm willing to pay the price, and I know that many other people are willing to pay the price too. If we're stagnating in life, we have to ask ourselves why we haven't been paying it.

Are we seeing progress? Are we using the goal formula to quantify if we're moving in the right direction? Or are we scared to even look? It has been said that many people are climbing the corporate ladder, only to find years later that the ladder is leaning against the wrong building (wrong meaning wrong for them). So I've got to be willing to be authentic with myself. I've got to be willing to confront my best thinking. I've got to be willing to go to any lengths to have the experience that I'm on this planet to have. Half-measures avail us nothing!

Some years ago there was a pretty smart person named Albert E.N. Gray, who gave a speech about "The Common Denominator of Success". He said that after having spent time studying successful people in his business and in various walks of life, he discovered that there is one common denominator of success that all successful people do. And this is it: Successful people are in the habit of doing things that failures don't like to do. That's what Albert said. And, it's not that successful people like doing these things, it's just that they do them anyway, because they subordinate their preferences (about what methods would be pleasant to them) to the result. The result is more important.

So it's not like the successful people are lucky, that they've been blessed with a liking for these things that failures don't like to do. They don't like to do them either. They just do them anyway, because their results are more important than being comfortable. And keep in mind that Albert said these people are in the *habit* of doing things that failures don't like to do. Again, consistency comes into play; being willing to develop new habits, new conditioning and new paradigms from which we operate on a habitual basis brings us the fruit.

By their fruits ye shall know them.
Matthew 7:16

A lot of people have a problem with successful people. I'll sometimes get a dirty look from an ignorant bystander when I roll up in a Maserati or a Bentley. A member of the victim society can't accept that they have created their own reality. Sometimes, if somebody has the wherewithal to ask me what it is that I do for a living, I'm sometimes tempted to say, "Oh, I just got lucky." But actually, if you want to know where my luck comes from, it comes from just being the most consistent and persistent person that I can possibly be. And because that's who I've chosen to be, there is no competition in my life. I can completely master any activity or undertaking that I choose to be involved with.

Now granted, there are not a whole lot of things that I'm involved in. I believe in *developing my strengths and managing my weaknesses.* I'm ignorant in most areas, but the few things that I do, I do extraordinarily well and I get a lot of satisfaction out of them. Quite often it's just a matter of persisting until I get the result that I'm seeking. And when I say persisting, I mean persisting regardless of circumstances. How else does someone develop a new skill? If you've got an interest in being good at golf you are going to hit a lot of golf balls.

At one point I was taking golf lessons. (My instructor's name was Chip. Believe it or not, that's really his name. He told me his brother's name was Putt.) This guy would put a ball down on the grass, take a swing, and hit the ball perfectly every time. He would give me instruction on my posture and all the little movements I was doing incorrectly, and then I would watch his example again. At one point I made a comment.

I said, "Man, every time you hit the ball it's absolutely perfect!" And his comment was, "Well, I've hit millions of golf balls."

Quality means doing it right when no one is looking.
Henry Ford (1863 – 1947)

So let's not be surprised when someone appears lucky. We know behind the scenes that every overnight success wasn't necessarily so. I've had the great pleasure on several occasions of being with Andy Andrews, the best-selling author of "The Traveler's Gift" and other books. If you've read the book, you know it's a masterpiece. Well, this guy got turned down, got rejected, by countless publishing houses before he could get this masterpiece of a book into the hands of the people who he knew would benefit from it. And now, of course, the cat's out of the bag. The guy's a best-selling author, but he had to persist.

I think of the story of Colonel Sanders, with his fried chicken idea that nobody wanted, and now look. I was touring the east coast of Australia recently. While in Newcastle, I was walking around the city streets, and what did I find? KFC. It's not a big town, but there it was. Could you imagine if everyone gave up when adversity showed up in their life? We wouldn't have anything. We would still be living in caves and rubbing sticks and stones to make fire. I heard that Thomas Edison had over 10,000 failed attempts at creating the incandescent light bulb as he was inventing it. Good thing he didn't give up.

So we make our own luck. When I think of my personal integrity as it relates to that statement, I think about holding my course and taking consistent action after any initial emotional euphoria from making the decision wears off. Yes, high integrity people are people that hold their course. And think of this: Who would you rather do business with? Someone who is demonstrating stability in their business practices and fulfills their promises, or someone who is all over the map? Who would you rather be in a relationship with? Ah, there is an interesting question. And are you that type of person? Do you have the self-discipline to hold your course after the honeymoon? The bottom line for me is *knowing who I am, and then being that.* Behaving that way, doing the things that person would do, and of course seeing the results show up in my life. And please note - this is not about being perfect, it's about being diligent and consistent.

But for the masses, luck is an easy sell. The lottery-mentality forever keeps people looking for something-for-nothing. Every time I'm in Las Vegas I see the old ladies sitting at the slot machines with their cigarettes and their hands jittering thinking that the next pull is going to be their big break. Are they ever going to get it? There are no free rides in life. The casinos weren't built on winners.

But it's an easy sell. Why else would people put countless millions of dollars into lottery programs and waiting by the TV at drawing time, and yelling at their kids if they're making any noise or watching a different channel, when they could be taking a self-reliant approach to their success? It's because most people believe that successful people are lucky, and that it's outside of their circle of influence to become successful themselves. Perhaps the gods of fate will smile on them. These same people, if presented with an opportunity to take action towards their own benefit, towards their own betterment, to take responsibility for their results in their life, turn those opportunities down with a statement like "It's too good to be true." Anything but take responsibility.

You know, when I first decided to write a book about personal integrity, responsibility and self-reliance, a thought came through my mind: "Oh no! You want to send millions of people running in the other direction? Just tell them they're responsible for their results." But I went through with it, so I guess I just can't stop myself from sharing what actually works in my life.

In fact, I remember a time when I was giving a business presentation to a group of about 300 people. I was explaining a marketing system that they could use to work from anywhere with a phone and computer and generate enough income to more than double what most of them were earning at their day jobs and create some options and freedom in their life. I explained how everything worked, I showed some historical and projected figures; I even had some people there who had already begun earning significant money with the system share their experiences. After the presentation, someone asked me, "If this is so good, why doesn't everybody do it?" I could sense that he had himself in a state of suspense over how I would answer this challenge he had laid down. And the most direct and efficacious answer that I could come up with in that moment was, "Because most people are idiots." Anyway, he got started with the business that day, as did many other people.

Most people say they want better financial results and yet when presented with a solution or opportunity that could dramatically improve one's situation, I have found that most people's initial reaction is that there must be something wrong, illegal or immoral about it. In fact, they'll seek out evidence to prove their beliefs. And as we know, we find what we seek. So people get to stay stuck.

When opportunity knocks, most people roll over and complain about the noise.

How many people are willing to admit that their own decisions have gotten them to where they are now? And how many people are really willing to risk looking bad? This is really what it comes down to. People often don't commit themselves to an opportunity to advance themselves because of fear of criticism from others. They trade their possibilities for the status quo.

But it remains unidentified as a cause for one's inaction and why they're not moving forward in their life. Instead of confronting their fears, they immediately start citing circumstances when presented with a new idea. I heard someone refer to this as the "but-eyes." "Yeah, but I _____ ." "Yeah, but I have this problem." "Yeah, but you don't understand. Here's my situation." And somehow they always see themselves as different from successful people. Their circumstances are in control of what they're able to do and what their possibilities are in their life. They're not at cause for their experience; they're at the effect of their circumstances. This is beyond crippling; this is "crash and burn".

Circumstance does not make the man; it reveals him to himself.
James Allen (1864 – 1912)

Now I understand, as I'm sure many people do, that we have things which require us to be flexible in our life. I've had periods of mourning and the emotional imbalance of grieving over a loss. Certainly we've all had circumstances. Any successful person has had circumstances that they had to and were willing to overcome. And did setbacks happen? Sure. But to be constantly identified with our circumstances and to speak of them as if they are preventing us from doing what we would like to do is a self-dooming conversation. And when I encounter people like that, and they are not hard to find, I know that they are not going to be taking any significant action in their life.

What these people also like to do is speak of their circumstances with the people in their immediate social circle of influence. They speak of their circumstances, typically complaining about their circumstances, with other people who will agree with them. They get to share stories of misfortune, proving how difficult everyone's life is, and everyone gets to go nowhere.

So the question is: Are you at cause for your experience or are you at the effect of your circumstances? Are you a creator or a victim? Are you here to enjoy the abundance of the earth and all the possible experiences that you can have or are you here to lock yourself in a prison indefinitely?

People are always blaming their circumstances for what they are. I don't believe in circumstances. The people who get on in this world are the people who get up and look for the circumstances they want, and, if they can't find them, make them.
George Bernard Shaw (1856 – 1950)

Another indicator that a person is not going to be taking resourceful action in their life is when they are confrontational with a mentor figure who offers them guidance. It's kind of like the rebellious adolescent who already knows everything. In one of my businesses we offer a cost-effective lead management solution that saves salespeople a lot of time and simplifies their marketing. And from time to time I'll hear something like, "Well, why do I have to use that system?" But it's not about "have to". That's typical thinking of the masses who live by someone else's agenda. That's "sheeple" talk. That's another way of saying, "I am not in control."

There was never a "have to" anywhere in the conversation. Don't people have a choice? I can't force people to make right decisions. No, you don't *have to* use my system. You don't *have to* become successful; you don't *have to* create wealth in your life; you don't *have to* do a damn thing. But you came to me. You asked how to get results. I answered.

But a victim has to find a way to fulfill their self-image of being a victim. Some people are only satisfied by being dissatisfied. I could throw $100,000 at the person and hit them on the side of the head with it and it would still be a problem. No one can help someone who doesn't want to help themselves.

There are potentially endless combinations of excuses that people can use to justify why they continue to live at the effect of life. I lived that way for much of my life. And every time I started making excuses, I stopped making progress. When I had finally become thoroughly disgusted with self-denial and broken promises to myself, and I started taking action in the face of my circumstances, I began realizing what an unfortunate state victimhood is. The only payoff in it for me was getting agreement from other members of the vast victim-society, passing time in idle conversation.

Once you've made your departure from victim-society, it becomes pretty obvious. Still, sometimes people actually expect me to buy their excuses. Probably because there are so many people whose word is worthless, now it's okay for theirs to be worthless too. But I'm an actual leader. I'm not here (on this planet) to agree with people about how hard their circumstances are, and how weak and helpless they are. I actually do the things that successful people for centuries have been telling us to do if we want to be successful. I really believe this stuff.

Your circumstances may be uncongenial, but they shall not long remain so if you but perceive an Ideal and strive to reach it.
James Allen (1864 – 1912)

What if you're currently faced with uncongenial circumstances in the area of money? Instead of sitting around worrying about money, why don't you figure out something that you can create? Your thinking can be at least as great of an asset as your time and your material assets. Do whatever you have to do. Take a look. There are people that I know who have sold furniture, even other people's furniture that had been discarded, to get started in businesses, to have working capital, to have the means to take some action, any action that will move them in the direction of their goals. What is it that you can do right now that you haven't been doing because of your circumstances?

Perhaps you want to find an established business model which will increase the speed and likelihood of your success. This has been advised by so many affluent people lately, like Donald Trump, Robert Kiyosaki, Bob Proctor, etc. This is what I did!

By the way, if you want to go in this direction and you're looking for the right company or opportunity to get started with, find one with a lot of parasites and complaints on the internet. Then you'll know that the people there are actually doing something and getting results. This is bound to attract naysayers, liars who think nothing of slander, "bottom-feeders" with a better deal, and "good Samaritans" on the web who want to save you from the treachery of that terrible company (and sell you their opportunity instead, which is, of course, better). You've got to be able to think for yourself.

Where no oxen are, the crib is clean...
Proverbs 14:4

More important than *what* business you do, is *who* you do it with, provided you are in alignment with the basic purpose of the business. Please keep that in mind when you are investing your time, effort and resources into any endeavor of importance.

I've said many times that the best investment I ever made was an investment in me. I bet on me. And you know, I've attracted other people into my life who also bet on themselves. My association with other self-reliant people has led to some great synergistic relationships. If you mingle with people who do not have a good dose of self-belief and personal integrity, you'll soon find yourself succumbing again to a victim-society, wondering why things aren't going well and blaming circumstances for your hardship. Anyway, that's where most people are, and in my company we're working every day to be at cause for changing that way of thinking. And I tip my hat to anyone or any organization which is willing to confront this reality, because it is one of escalating severity. Victimhood doesn't just stay at home. It's like a virus that infects large populations.

There are those who argue that free enterprise is one of the last freedoms in America, and yet most of our population is so conned by the false prophets in the mass media (TV, newspapers, Internet) and by generations of security worshiping parents, that they can't even recognize opportunity, let alone take personal action. Having not accepted responsibility for our own results we have now gotten to the point where we have a society that is quick to give away their rights by allowing countless laws to be created in the name of security. As Ben Franklin said:

Those who would give up essential liberty to purchase a little temporary safety, deserve neither liberty nor safety.
Benjamin Franklin (1706 – 1790)

I feel this book is important because for us to be able to cultivate some sanity on this planet we've got to have conscious people who are able to take care of themselves. When the population is woken up to the point where it will no longer tolerate (or invite) government intrusion on the basic liberties of people, control mechanisms, bureaucracy, corporatism (what many people are calling fascism), then we can begin to heal as a human race. But as long as people are in this coma of denial and unconsciousness, freedom will continue to lose ground. This is an urgent thing.

I realize that I'm addressing Americans now, but this is not a strictly American phenomenon. As a freedom-loving American who actually believes in the "land of opportunity", this strikes a nerve in me. If you're an American reading this, know that we have an opportunity to be an example of freedom for all. We will do this by cultivating the self-reliance that Emerson implored us to adopt in the 1800's. We will not do this by remaining fat, arrogant, lazy and stupid. We can no longer continue to embarrass ourselves in the world market. We will not succeed if we continue to destroy ourselves from within, with endless litigation, victim thinking and never ending doses of poison from the media.

What's worse - to be face down in the dirt with the boot of oppression on our back, or to be face down in the dirt with no boot on our back?

Opportunity is knocking. Is anyone home?

-Simple Action-

Keep a personal journal and develop the habit of writing in it each day. There are three things to write about: Your challenges for the day, your wins for the day, and what you learned that day by studying whatever you've been studying. Be sure to identify what role you played in whatever challenges you faced, and how you can now be a part of the solution.

The magnitude of this action may not be apparent to you at first, but before long you will realize that you are writing the best self-help book ever written. I have looked back on journal entries I had written years earlier, and have been reminded of great discoveries that served me then and serve me again today.

Seek an opportunity that will assist you in fulfilling your vision for yourself. For example, if you envision a stronger, healthier body, find a health club that suits your objectives or buy some exercise equipment. If you've decided that you will live a more abundant lifestyle, find a competent financial advisor or seek a business opportunity. Learn what there is to learn, and after educating yourself, make a decision and take action.

It's Not Okay

The moment I decided to write this book was when I had just finished reading another book, from yet another best-selling self-help author, telling people to just feel good, use positive thinking and to learn to be okay with things the way they are. That it's okay to compromise on your goals and to be mediocre, and somehow that's "going with the flow". After more than 20 years of studying personal development I have become a bit sensitive to when someone wastes my time with a bunch of empty advice and misdirection that I've heard 10 billion friggin times. But I guess there's a pretty big market for this kind of shit.

Let me ask you, do you prefer to have an okay relationship with your loved ones, or a great relationship with your loved ones? Are you willing to compromise your health? Is it okay that you're constantly looking at the price tags on things? Is it okay to live a life of excuses, because you don't earn enough money to provide the lifestyle that you would really want? (Well, who needs all that nice stuff anyway?)

But it's not about need! It's about having choices. I choose to have choices. I choose not to live a life of concession. To me, that's not okay.

Understand that choosing to live in passive acceptance is not the way to self-actualization, or mastery, or happiness. For those who refuse to accept responsibility for their results, compromise and mediocrity is an easy sell. Maybe I'm just a total nonconformist. Maybe it's just because the masses are living the way they are that I'm so passionate about creating excellence in my life. Am I just a rebel? If the masses were all outrageously successful, would I want to be a loser? I don't think so.

And be not conformed to this world: but be ye transformed by the renewing of your mind, that ye may prove what is that good, and acceptable, and perfect, will of God.
Romans 12:2

The thing that struck me when I read that book was the idea that it's somehow spiritual to accept a lack of results in certain areas of your life. That it may be God's will for you to be broke (for example), and you can be okay with that, because you're getting by in these other areas. You're not beating your wife. You're a good parent. You try hard to watch what you eat and not be 10,000 pounds overweight. So it's okay to be a miserable failure in these other areas of your life, because look, you're good at these things here.

I am here to say, with the biggest, loudest, most thunderous voice I can, "IT'S NOT OKAY!" If you intend to get anywhere in your life, if you believe anything that we've been talking about here in terms of being a person who is able to fulfill your desires, that your vision for yourself is actually God's will for you, then no, it's not @#$%^&* okay that you're not getting the result that you say you want.

I think of some of the great achievers in recent history - Thomas Edison for example. When I think of Edison, I think of the tremendous dissatisfaction he had with contemporary technology. This drive was at cause for all his inventions that we all benefit from now. *It wasn't okay* that he had to light candles every day to see where the hell he was going in the middle of the night. *Not okay!*

It's not okay to be sick, broke and miserable, because you're "creative". It's not okay to be fat, miserable and contemptuous if you've got money. Success is the total package! It's not pick-and-choose. That's just more *lack* type thinking. It's not: "I can have this *or* this." Look, we've got more ability than we can possibly utilize in this lifetime. So what is it that I have to choose from?

Now, I'm not talking about being ridiculous and saying, "I can be a brain surgeon *and* an astronaut." Or "I can be a race horse jockey *and* a pro wrestler." These combinations obviously don't work. But I don't know that there was ever an astronaut who simultaneously wanted to be a brain surgeon, or a horse jockey (what do those guys weigh, 80 pounds?) who dreamed of being a smack-down champion. It just wasn't in them. But there is *something* in them. And if it's the pro wrestler, be the best damn pro wrestler in the world.

There is no excuse for failing to live out your purpose, and there is no honor in "I tried". It's called self-denial. *That's* what that is. It's ugly! It's not okay!

There are countless books on the shelf, possibly right next to this one if you bought it at a book store, that are going to be written by people who are not getting results that you would want in your life. They are not demonstrating success in their own life, and they think the way to happiness is for you to conform to your environment, because this is what they do. This approach probably sells a lot of books. After years of studying spirituality, personal development, business success, relationships, etc., I've discovered that there are a great deal of teachings that will lead you nowhere, because the expert (the seminar host, the author, the whatever) does not have experiential knowledge of the true ways of success. They are theorizing only, or regurgitating what they heard someone else did, and somehow that makes them an expert. I don't learn from people who just theorize. I look for the results of a philosophy before I decide if I'm going to apply it, or if I'm going to learn what *not* to do by observing that teaching.

A "therapy" which teaches that Man should adapt himself to his environment, rather than adapt the environment to him, is such a slave philosophy and is not workable - only because it is quite the reverse from truth.
L. Ron Hubbard (1911–1986)

So it's important to choose well whose advice you allow to shape your beliefs. And make no mistake about it; it will shape your beliefs. Perhaps you've noticed that there seems to be an ever-increasing group of people talking about creating wealth these days. Why? Because many people who had previously yielded to a belief that they had to accept living in deficit and mediocrity are now starting to look for direction and questioning old beliefs.

In terms of personal development, in terms of finding a mentor, in terms of choosing people to take advice from (and which to observe to find the contrast of what *not* to do), here is one thing I'll say: If the teaching does not embrace the reality of man's natural tendency to be abundant, they don't know anything about personal development. If you pick up a book and you read that it's okay for you to be broke because you tried hard, or you did okay in this other area of your life, or any kind of nonsense like that, don't put the book on the shelf, don't give it away, don't sell it on eBay, throw it in the friggin garbage. Do society a favor and have one less of those books on the planet. It's not okay.

Man was born to be rich, or grow rich by use of his faculties, by the union of thought with nature.
Ralph Waldo Emerson (1803 – 1882)

Let's pull our heads out of the mud and realize that we *are* powerful in our use of thought, that we *can* have it all, and that *by design* we were created in the image and likeness of who? That's correct. Therefore, what can't be done? What possibilities are not real for you? Well, they're the ones that you allow others to convince you are not real for you. Run in the other direction from that kind of thinking.

Now, of course, this requires us to think; and as I've been saying throughout this book, this is not comfortable. Most people close their ears when they hear the truth or something that goes against what their comfortable believe system is. If it makes people uncomfortable that I'm challenging their traditional beliefs, so be it. I would say I'm sorry, but I'm not.

As I mentioned before, I have a company where we teach marketing strategies to people who say they want to accelerate their income. Thousands of people throughout the world contact us to inquire about our program. We've proven that we can teach virtually anyone with some drive and a willingness to learn how to earn over $20,000 per month working less than 20 hours per week. It's all very simple. 100% of the people who contact us do so because they are not getting the financial results they want. And yet, 97% of the people who have a curiosity about how they can become successful (and that's about as far as it goes is a curiosity) do absolutely nothing with the information. We freely give the information, but 97% of people hit a wall when confronted with a new idea or an opportunity to take action.

Everybody wants to be somebody; nobody wants to grow.
Johann Wolfgang von Goethe (1749 – 1832)

After all, if people actually took advantage of opportunities that showed up in their life they would no longer be able to play victim. Then what would they have to talk about with their friends, family and neighbors? Definitely not comfortable.

And the media confirms that this is okay. You get to see countless examples of failure and victimhood on the news. You get to see Jerry Springer and shows like "Cops", where people are living at sub-animal levels. Apparently, it's not uncommon. And because I've been removed from that sort of TV viewing for years now, I'm sometimes shocked when I see what's happening in society. I think, "My goodness, are people actually living like this?"

My wife went to visit some people she hadn't seen in a long time, people from her past, and spent a few days in the area where they live. She used to live there herself. She called me on the phone during her trip and she made a comment, "You know John, no one here lives like we do." She was startled by the contrast between the lifestyle that we've created for ourselves, and that of those who have made no such demands on life.

Right now, networking websites are popular. People get to create little web pages about themselves and network with others. So I recently decided to look up some people that I knew from my youth and see if I could find them on the web. Of the few I did find, most of them were at least as bad off as they were 20 years ago when I knew them. And after making a little web page of my own, some people from my past contacted me. Invariably, when they discover that I've made tremendous progress in my life they make some comment like, "Wow, you've done really well for yourself." And when I expose them to how I did it, they reply with something like, "I could only dream of being that successful", if they reply at all. Like

I'm special. Like I'm some kind of celebrity or something. They instinctively separate themselves from the "successful" person.

Sometimes in casual conversation someone will ask me if I heard what so-and-so did, or if I know about so-and-so (and they cite some gossip about a famous person); and I'll say, "No; *do they know me?*" And they chuckle, because they're assuming that the person wouldn't. Perhaps they think that because they have a casual relationship with me (which they don't have with the celebrity) that somehow we're in the same group, and the celebrity is in a different group, and therefore how could they know me? There is an implied separation.

This phenomenon, which I call *celebrityism*, is one way people set themselves up as part of the masses - part of the working class. Mass-media helps you do this every day, as does our educational system which also induces separatist thinking and very successfully produces a working-class. That's what it's designed to do - to produce conformists, cheap labor for the system. Make no mistake about it.

So don't think like an outsider when you encounter someone who has gained recognition for their accomplishments. They are simply living their chosen purpose. Many of the people who I think are spectacular are not necessarily popular in modern 21st-century pop-culture. (And many have left the planet already.) But if I was to have an opportunity to meet them I would understand that we're just having a human interaction. We're all of the same source anyway, so there's nothing to freak out about. When I think of esteemed people I think of people like Ben Franklin, Ralph Emerson, Jesus of Nazareth, Swami Muktananda, Gandhi and Napoleon Hill. So there are a few examples. I don't hear any star-struck teenage girls screaming in my head right now as I say these names to myself.

And how about John Lavenia? Now, take my name out of that sentence and put your name in there. How about you? There is so much opportunity for us to make examples of ourselves - to leave a legacy. If not you, then who? Why wouldn't you be included in the list of highly successful or impactful or influential people on this planet? If someone with the mental state of even a Hitler could be so influential, why couldn't you?

Think about that. I remember hearing somewhere about a list of the most influential people in the history of the world, and at one time, according to whomever the experts are, Adolf Hitler was in the top five. Jesus was number one, and I think William Shakespeare was number three. Yea, how about Shakespeare? There's a guy I would like to meet.

But the media teaches us to be apart from the few successful people – the famous, the powerful, the rich. And whether we realize it or not, the message is often that it's bad to be rich. This is an easy to sell to the public. You can find example after example where people are criticizing the rich entrepreneur, the wealthy actor or sports-hero, or the "big bad company" exploiting the poor, helpless people. Sometimes it's very obvious, and sometimes it's very subtle. Think of the movies that you go to. I remember hearing a line in one big Hollywood blockbuster film that went, "We may not be rich, but we're honest." This is an easy sell. Now keep in mind, the people making the movies aren't broke. Sony/Columbia Pictures isn't struggling with money. They know they'll get *your* money if they can get your agreement, and the idea that rich people are bad and poor people are good and "honest" is an easy sell. You've got to be awake when you watch movies or TV programming. I know for myself that I am willing to personally reinterpret every idea that is shown to me on that screen.

Lack of money is the root of all evil.
George Bernard Shaw (1856 – 1950)

How easy it is to find criticisms about visionaries like Bill Gates or Oprah. People who are performing at the top of their game and kicking ass financially are easy targets for the critics. And of course, the critics don't get very good results. Some people, in looking for evidence to back up their idea that there is nobility in poverty, will point to people who have dedicated their life to charitable service to humanity, even though these people demonstrated more *real* prosperity consciousness in their time here on this planet than most people could even imagine. Think about it, being able to walk into any place in any country with full knowing that they could acquire whatever is required to get done what needs to get done. They could show up with the clothes on their back knowing that the details were handled, and have always been handled; and that, my friends, is prosperity consciousness - transcending labels of "mine" or "not mine". So there is no virtue in poverty. There is no compromise.

But again, this is not ordinary thinking. And the purpose of the herd is *to keep you in the herd*. I know I'm on a rant now, but listen to this. I was reading about a European tourist that was visiting America. This person happened to be an automobile enthusiast, and when asked what he thought about driving in America he said, "It's dangerous." And when asked why he thought it was dangerous he replied, "It's the speed! Americans drive so painfully slow that the mind goes to sleep." In a progressive society, the competent set the pace. In a conforming society, the incompetent set the pace. So we get laws forcing us to lower the bar again. Moving on…

There is one more piece of conventional "wisdom" that I would like to address here, because although it is terribly subtle, it's disastrous. And it's this: People have developed a fear-based belief that any help they receive from another individual is actually an attempt to hurt them or scam them or mislead them. This is a devastating belief to have, but it's one that's been perpetuated for generations. It is perpetuated not only in the sphere of personal interaction, as people prove dishonest and take advantage of each other, but also in the larger sphere of organizations and governments, which demonstrate a staggering lack of integrity, and are, of course, made up of people.

This is why our personal integrity is so important. This is bigger than just you or me. When we ignore principles, live dishonestly and refuse to accept responsibility in our lives, we become part of the problem for everyone.

Liberty means responsibility. That is why most men dread it.
George Bernard Shaw (1856 – 1950)

People have tried to give away the responsibility for their health to the medical system, and look what it's gotten them. I got a letter in the mail from a major bank that was offering a new credit card to its customers (oh boy!), and printed on the envelope was, "51% of Americans take at least one prescription drug each day. Now, you can save money on the prescriptions you need when you use the new such-and-such credit card!" Isn't this great?! Sickness and poverty-consciousness all in one! What a deal.

How about the 10,000% increase in autistic spectrum disorder over the last few years. Is that a coincidence?

And do you want to really get ugly? How about the millions of CHILDREN who are now on psychiatric drugs to treat an ever growing list of "mental disorders" that didn't even exist when I was a child? Where did these "disorders" come from?

People give away the responsibility for their income to their job. They give the responsibility for their spirituality to the church. They give the responsibility for their government to politicians. And how's that working out? How do you like working to pay out half your earnings in taxes? And what kind of American would come up with something like the "Patriot Act"? Did someone secretly change the lyrics of our national anthem to end with, "…the former land of the free, and once home of the brave"?

This is what happens when we blindly follow the herd, which would opt for TV zombification before accepting responsibility. Control is snatched up by authoritarians and bureaucrats who are obsessed with it.

How many people can honestly say that they trust their government to act in their best interest, or even to act in the best interest of the human race or the planet? Look at the destruction that's committed in the name of "freedom". When did liberation come to mean control? Here comes another war. And when it's all done, we get to count the bodies, load the oil tankers and put up the fast-food signs. Are the locals glad we "helped" them? Whether we know it or not, witnessing this hypocrisy adds to the belief that we should beware of anyone displaying goodwill.

We do not have to visit a madhouse to find disordered minds; our planet is the mental institution of the universe.
Johann Wolfgang von Goethe (1749 – 1832)

I saw a television advertisement just the other day when I was in a store. A company was advertising how they are helping the war veterans from the latest invasion of another country by America, in this case Iraq. It pictured a young man of African descent, perhaps 18 years old, in a wheelchair, with no legs. I think it's grotesquely bizarre that we accept the reality of an 18-year-old man missing his legs, plain for all to see on daytime television, and somehow this is okay in the name of controlling another country. What kind of a world is this where this is okay? I'll say it again in case you missed it: This young man had no legs!

I don't know what else to say. Am I just an idealist to think that it doesn't have to be this way? The image made me sick. And it wasn't my son. It wasn't anybody that I know. Was that your son? When will it be your son?

Now we can sit on the sidelines and let the bureaucrats and psychopaths continue to run the world while we nod in agreement with the media and distract ourselves with drugs, diet fads and celebrity gossip, or we can embrace the urgency of this and win the integrity of our nations back by having a unified voice based in some semblance of sanity.

How do we begin? We begin on a personal level. It starts with *personal* integrity. We've got to be willing to *authentically be of service* to other people. When we are on-purpose we help ourselves and we help our fellow man, *and* we become willing to *receive* help from our fellow man. This brings people together, and the divide-and-conquer strategy loses ground.

I choose to be part of the solution. I'll do this, if by no other way, by fulfilling the purpose of why I'm here. By not living in self-denial, and by acknowledging my greatness, I can now acknowledge your greatness. And I'm more than willing to accept your help. Would you please help me by being the best that you can be in fulfilling your life's purpose? Would you think for yourself and communicate with others in a way that causes them to think for themselves? Would you help me get the message out that people *can* be powerful in their lives, and that they *are* at cause for their experience? Then we can have a whole different experience; an experience of a society that works, and that loves and respects each other. We'll do this by waking up to our gross inconsistencies with basic rational behavior. And don't just help me, help yourself. This is your world too, and it's your children's world. Yes, your son's legs may depend on it. In fact, the future of our human race *does* depend on it.

-Simple Action-

Give a great personal-development book to 10 people you know. I'd like to tell you to give them this book, but I think that would be a little arrogant. There are many books that I would recommend if you like. You can see a list of suggested reading in the back of this book, or for an expanded list visit www.JohnLavenia.com

Eliminate TV, newspapers and FM radio for at least 90 days. If you happen to hear or see conformity-inducing programming, remember the agenda of those who publish it, and reinterpret it as such. Don't worry about missing something important; if the aliens are landing, you'll see the spaceships. Don't be surprised if you never want to go back. Music is fine (as long as it's not country music (just kidding)). Movies are fine too, as long as you remember to keep your brain working. If you want to entertain yourself *and* get your brain going, I recommend movies like "The Matrix", "V for Vendetta" and "Idiocracy".

You Are The Answer

For years I've heard self-help speakers say that abundance and success is the natural state of things. And for years I wasn't observing this in my life. I worked arduously in a never ending mire of complication, always wanting for fulfillment, happiness and abundance but never being able to *work hard enough* to get it. And I had deferred the things in life that I was passionate about for some brighter day, in the name of "responsibility". Where did I get the belief that I couldn't have passion, fun, abundance and responsibility all at the same time? Have you ever experienced this? Keep this in mind as you read this chapter.

The height of mastery is simplicity.

It was about nine o'clock in the morning when I arrived in Sydney. Because it was so early, my suite at the hotel was not yet prepared for my arrival. So I wandered up to the top floor executive lounge to have some refreshment and read about what was going on locally. After deciding on a day trip to the zoo and a bridge walk, I got into the business section of some of the local newspapers. Having a mind for business, I figured I could learn something.

There were many articles about local entrepreneurs and new business startups. Some of which were fairly interesting, but there was a recurring theme that kept showing up: Business is complicated. Now, I don't claim to be a know-it-all when it comes to business (or anything else for that matter) but I could clearly see that either the columnists who were writing the articles or the people they were interviewing had a dogmatic and linear approach to business.

Most of the talk was about business planning, incremental increase in market share and all the minute moving parts that are going into getting this business or that business off the ground. Terribly complicated, and for me, terribly uninteresting. I ended that experience with the feeling that if I were a salaried worker, I would be better off remaining as one. And since that's most people, I guess that's who the paper is written for.

I remember back when I was in school, I dreaded my trigonometry class. I remember looking at the equations and feeling all the energy drain out of my body. I would actually fall asleep sometimes. I was so confused by all of it. It didn't seem real to me. I had no interest in it. It seemed completely worthless in my life. And, of course, that's because it *was* completely worthless in my life. Interest renders aptitude. And since I had no interest, I had no aptitude.

But I wanted to do well. I knew that I wasn't a dumb person. I was doing very well in other areas, but the curriculum said that smart people did trigonometry. I assumed that there must have been some very qualified experts who put this curriculum together. After all, other people were doing trigonometry. Why wasn't I? Maybe I just wasn't qualified for success like my peers?

This is probably how many potentially great business people feel when they read the business section of a newspaper, like I did that day in Sydney. There's so much to know. There's so much content, and it's written by the experts! Maybe I can't be successful because I'm not like these superheroes who seem to know so much. Let's put the brakes on that train of thought for a moment.

Obviously, there is a need for specialized knowledge to accomplish various things in life - accounting, nuclear physics, and maybe even trigonometry. But I have never met a highly successful person who knows *all* the knowledge necessary to operate their own business! In fact, the biggest know-it-alls that have crossed my path have been the small players. (And at times I have been one of them!) The common thinking of the high achievers has been *conceptual*. That is to say that creative thought, which leads to success, comes from a concept or a vision that a person has unequivocally adopted.

Some of the most profound things in life are the most simple. I can think of many times, and I'm sure you can too, when a few words or a simple phrase changed your perspective on an important situation. Agitation does not equal effectiveness. Mental activity run amok does not equal thinking.

So here's a simple question: What do you want? You know, most people have a really hard time honestly answering that question. Originating a creative thought is one of the highest functions that a human is capable of. And yet, this is what is necessary if we are going to be able to answer that question. Otherwise, we will resort to regurgitating some traditional and seemingly reasonable belief of what we "should" want. When we do this, we are, in fact, at the effect of other people's thinking. Other people's beliefs make for rather limp motivators.

If I'd asked people what they wanted, they would have asked for a better horse.
Henry Ford (1863 – 1947)

I'm an avid reader. For some reason, I've been on an intellectual path all of my life. Other people might be the devotional or emotional type, or into dancing, or banging on tambourines and chanting, or whatever. And that's great, but I'm an intellectual. I love to study. I love to understand how things work. Why things work. How things don't work.

And this takes a lot of work. I don't know how or when I chose this, but here I am. The good news about this is that I can now explain things pretty well for other people to get a basic understanding. The challenging side to all this is that I can easily complicate things, and I can be at the effect of that which I read or heard.

I remember once when I was consulting with a group of business associates about how to increase sales closing ratios. After much discussion and opinion, we decided to create a system that we felt would create more effectiveness in our business efforts. It had a lot of moving parts. It had to be executed perfectly, and it involved a major variable: Other people. After weeks of implementation, countless hours of training, painstakingly evaluating results, etc., we scrapped the idea and went back to basics. Like the famous coach Vince Lombardi used to say, "Blocking and tackling." This is what wins the game.

So part of the price of blindly adopting the beliefs and opinions of others is that you get to add complications on your path to whatever it is that you want. But the realization of our desires requires that we learn some things, so there has to be some balance here. The question then is: What to believe? Who to believe?

Just trust yourself, then you will know how to live.
Johann Wolfgang von Goethe (1749 – 1832)

I offer that the first and most profound answer is to believe in yourself. Yes, *you are so capable!* And you will augment that self-belief by associating yourself with the thinking of others who also believe in themselves.

Think of how the brain works. It pulls information from all different experiences, memories, things that you've studied, things that are memorable that stick out in your mind, etc. And this happens all the time. In fact, the most challenging thing for me about writing this book was just making it all flow, because I have so many ideas flying around in there. If you want to personally experience what that looks like, come to one of my seminars.

But how this can benefit us is that if we simply saturate ourselves with right-thinking material, if we keep immersing ourselves into the teachings of the great achievers, the masters, people whose life works, and we consistently and repetitiously keep good information in front of us, then in the moment of truth, we'll have the benefits of that. Because where is our mind going? It's going to what we are habitually thinking about.

So let's "load our guns" with good ammo. Have the books for yourself and your family. Have the audio recordings in your automobile or in your stereo system. In fact, put aside a separate bank account for education to continue. This works wonders for people in their feeling of self-worth and their confidence. One of the greatest ways and one of the simplest ways to build a person's self-esteem, to build your self-esteem, is to learn something new every day. So education beyond (and especially beyond) what the public school or university curriculum is willing to teach you is so beneficial.

This strong self-belief is so vital. Part of the reason why many people don't demonstrate success in their life is because of celebrityism, which I introduced in the preceding chapter - the idea that the few successful people that they get to see on television, or the odd person in their social group whose life happens to work, is different than them. People seem to automatically identify themselves as being different than "the successful people". Therefore there is an imaginary wall of demarcation between themselves and who they think the successful people are. But if we look at some of the organizations on our planet that have gotten great results in the area of empowering people, they are ones that are principle driven, and the principals have an underlying foundation of unity.

A great example of this would be 12-step fellowships. The reason that 12-step fellowships work is because as soon as a person who is in the grips of their addiction shows up in a 12-step fellowship, they are *a part of* instead of *apart from*. They are able to relate with others who are also on that same path and they are empowered by being understood and by understanding. They are empowered by the oneness of the group, the singularity of purpose that binds the group together. We could say that anything that creates unity is beneficial and productive. Anything that creates separatism or dissension is counterproductive. And this correlates directly with leadership, who I am willing to learn from and who I choose to associate with in my life.

Knowing that many of my greatest breakthroughs in life have come through interaction with other people - messengers who have shown up in my life, role models - it's a good idea to surround ourselves with opportunities for breakthrough interactions. We can choose to put ourselves in an environment that's going to accelerate our growth. In fact, nothing will accelerate our growth faster than choosing the right environment.

If I have seen further it is by standing on the shoulders of Giants.
Sir Isaac Newton (1643 – 1727)

Now, I'm not talking about joining social groups or committees where you've got a bunch of people with egos that need to be fed self-importance. We must maintain our self-reliance. I think committees are fabulous if you want to kill some time while you prepare for old age. I think committees are a great study of how to get the least amount done in the most amount of time. So I'm not a big fan of committees. That's not the environment that I'm talking about.

What I'm talking about is identifying other individuals who are also on the path that you're on and who have accrued personal victories that inspire you, and putting yourself in their path. Show up at events where successful people are. Be willing to serve. Perhaps volunteer or take an intern position part-time to be in the presence of people who have mastered what you say you want to do. Be willing to ask for some of that person's time. I'm happy to buy lunch for someone who has been where I want to go and who can illuminate the path a bit.

Now, when seeking mentors or role models, understand this looks nothing like celebrityism. Do not accost your potential mentor like the paparazzi on the entry ramp to the Academy Awards. Whenever I am seeking counsel from someone else, I always go into the interaction with the thought of, "How can I serve them?" I believe in synergistic relationships. I don't just think of what I can get, but what I can give as well. And knowing that you have the potential to reach equally great heights or even greater heights than this mentor, you are now their peer. You are both experiencing your humanness right now, and therefore there is no need for rank or groveling or feeling intimidated because you're both just a couple of spirits having a temporary human experience, and that's it.

I have no problem having a conversation with anyone if they're approaching me as a peer - another person hanging out on this planet for a little while looking to have a great life experience. When people acknowledge and are respectful of other people's space, and they understand that time is precious for everyone, then it's always a great interaction. I'm happy to spend time with those people. But when somebody is demanding or groveling or "needing help" or demeaning or disrespectful of another person's space, nobody wants to be in that environment for long.

This has to be especially true for celebrities and public figures. No wonder the saying exists that it's lonely at the top. Most people won't let successful people just be. So if you want to be a "successful people" go ahead and be like them, acknowledge that you are already one of them, and do unto them as you would have them do unto you.

Get clear right now that you *are* the next big success, top producer, high achiever, or whatever it is that you're looking for. The main difference between you and those who have already been recognized as having done it is time. If you're in action now, time is on your side, and you have no competition.

When I host introductory business trainings or presentations I explain various marketing techniques, advertisements, scripts, and things that I've used to generate wealth in my life and my business. Because it's very common that people think competitively, sometimes the question comes up, "How is it that you can give all this information to people, aren't you afraid that they'll become your competition?" Or something like this, "Well, if everybody did what you are saying to do, then the market would be saturated. How can you give this information? Obviously you're not worried about it."

But the reality is that there is no competition. If we come from the idea that there is plenty for everyone, a prosperity conscious position, then we don't fear competition, because we know that competition is a self-defeating idea and that there is no shortage of supply in the world. There is no shortage of wealth; there is only a shortage of ideas.

There is yet another, more tangible reason to not fear competition, and that is that quite often people aren't going to take action! There is no competition for the man or woman of action. Multi-billionaires could hand out free business advice, and still most people are just not going to do what they are shown to do. This is how successful people continue to be a small minority. This is one of the causes for why the middle-class is dwindling in America. 97% of the time people are not going to do what they need to do to get the results that they say they want. So there is no competition.

In times of change, learners inherit the Earth, while the learned find themselves beautifully equipped to deal with a world that no longer exists.
Eric Hoffer (1902 – 1983)

Think about this. There are a few variants out there in the world about what people are calling "The Law of Compensation". One definition is that, very simply, money is reward for service rendered. Okay, that's a pretty simple idea. If you want to earn more money, provide a higher level of service. Okay fine, but there is a compensation formula that I resonate with which I think greatly illuminates this law. This was explained to me by a guy who had earned millions of dollars before I knew what millions of dollars even looked like. His name is Bob Proctor, and it goes like this.

My income will be in direct correlation to three points, three factors. Number one is the need or the demand for what I do, for the service that I provide. Number two is my ability to provide that service. And number three is the difficulty that there would be in replacing me. Those three things - the demand for what I provide, my ability to provide, and the difficulty there would be if I had to be replaced - that would determine my income.

So let's think about that. The first thing is the demand. Everyone is familiar with the concept of supply and demand, right? Whatever business you're in, there is obviously a demand for what you do or you would have never gone down that road in the first place. And you likely had no part in creating that demand. It's just the fact that you showed up here on this planet at this time in an environment where that demand exists. You get to be the beneficiary of that opportunity. Wonderful! So the first part you have very little to do with.

The second part is where you come in. This is where diligence happens. This is where you become the best that you can be at whatever it is you've chosen to do with your time here. You get to develop mastery in this area of service that you're providing. Now think about the great leaders of business, the shining examples of innovation, and the champions of sport. Think about Tiger Woods. Do you think he has a part-time approach to his golf playing? No, he's a golfer. That's who he is in his essence. He is 100% a golfer, and so he golfs, and he develops that skill in a way that obviously most people would think is unreasonable. But there he goes.

I recently started playing the guitar. I have a passion for music, so I decided to take up a new instrument. So I bought a new guitar, and it's my intention to have this thing sound good, so I decided to learn as much as I can, as fast as I can. I'm taking various courses and I'm learning from people who are masters of the instrument, and they've been playing for 25 years. Some of these people are playing 10 hours a day. They are guitarists. That's who they are, and they're the best. So my ability to provide the service is where I come in.

And the third thing is the difficulty there would be in replacing me. Well, it doesn't take a genius to walk around and see that there are not a whole lot of diligent people. Here is an example, let's say that you want to get yourself a cup of coffee. You're driving in your car, you decide you want coffee, and you stop at the convenience store (here in the United States we've got 7-Eleven, Circle-K and others). You go into the convenience store and you get your cup of coffee, self-serve of course, and you go to the front counter. The clerk at the front counter rings it up and says in a gruff voice, "Is that it?" You pay your 89 cents and off you go with your coffee. You get to have a mediocre cup of coffee, and it was expeditious and inexpensive, and that was the whole experience.

Okay, now let's say it's the next day and you want to have a cup of coffee. You're driving in your car and you decide to stop at Starbucks (they're pretty much everywhere now). So you pull into the Starbucks parking lot, and the first thing you have to do is find a parking spot, because the place is packed. You park your car, you go inside and you get to wait in line with the other customers.

While you're waiting in line you're gazing upon all these wonderful accessories for your coffee loving experience (various cups and espresso makers and novelties) and then you get to the counter and the barista greets you. Now you've got to decide whether you want the Venti Sugar-free Vanilla Latte or the Tall Double Shot Espresso Part-skim Cappuccino. And there's lots of game in this. There's lots of opportunity for you to feel like you're part of the experience. There's an opportunity for you to express yourself here.

After the barista greets you, you order your drink (in my case, a Grande Nonfat Latte) and then the barista asks you what your name is so they can make sure that your name goes on that creation that they are about to make specifically for you, fresh of course. And then they say, "Well sir, would you like a scone or perhaps a muffin to accompany your latte today?" You answer, and after completing payment, you get to anticipate receiving your order, ultimately getting your coffee which is proudly delivered in the very fashionable Starbucks cup, and off you go.

It was a completely different experience! There is no competition! Think about the difference between those two experiences. That's why people are willing to wait in line to pay 1000% markup (don't mark me on the numbers here) for a product that is certainly excellent, but also for an experience of high-level service for which there is no competition. Now of course, other coffee companies have caught on to this business model and are racing to catch up, but Starbucks has conquered the coffee industry.

So think about that. Am I willing to be the best at what I do? There is a Sanskrit term called Dharma, which basically means *purpose in life.* The idea of Dharma is that you've got a certain drive, a desire, an expression of talent and ability that resides in you, and that no one else in the world has that exact ability or expression of that talent. So you've been divinely guided to develop this specific area. What we can do is ask ourselves if we are willing to be the best at that, and are we willing to look at ways that we can use our abilities and our talents to better serve our fellow man.

For myself, I have been drawn to studying personal development and applying it into my life to an ever-increasing extent for over 20 years. And after 20 years of study and application, I've become a pretty competent teacher of it because the principles are alive in me. I've gained experiential knowledge of how things work in my life and in the lives of others. I've gained wisdom by applying the knowledge that I've been studying. So this book is an expression of my ability to teach others the principles as they work in my life.

This is something people have been asking me to do for years, and perhaps because of my old paradigm, my old self image, my old idea that "I'm not worthy" or "who am I to be a leader at this level", I had procrastinated. I had been in a state of indecision about writing this book. But hey, I'm a teacher. I teach these principles. That's who I've become. For some reason it keeps showing up in my life. And it's effortless! And people love it. They come to my seminars and teleconferences by the thousands. So what the hell was I doing holding off on something that seems so obvious? Sometimes we're not able to see things about ourselves that seem obvious to others. It can be of great benefit to speak with people who we have a loving an honest relationship with about our intentions and our direction in life. These would be people who have no personal interest in suppressing or invalidating others because they already have a solid belief in themselves. But we may be reluctant to do this at times, especially if we've often been invalidated or in the frequent company of "armchair quarterbacks".

This is a funny visual. Here in America there are a lot of people who love to watch football on TV, and out of this ritual a new classification of person has emerged called the armchair quarterback. These people always have great advice (as they're screaming at the television about what the athletes on the field should have done) as they sit there 50 pounds overweight, drinking alcohol and whatever else, and gorging themselves with carbohydrates. I know this is an extreme example, but I also know that in daily life people are quick to talk about their opinions on anything and everything. So most times it's a good practice to keep our own counsel. But to get an objective view from and of myself was something that took the willingness to put progress in front of my preferences. I had to become willing to subordinate my preference for being comfortable to my willingness to evolve and make progress.

This requires that I remain awake to how I occur in the lives of others. Clearly, my Dharma directly relates to how I am able to serve others with the strengths that I have developed. And still, I must also remember that I am the one who ultimately knows my purpose, my passion and the most resourceful expression of it. I am the one who must ultimately choose my course. Once I choose a course, I hold that course and I build momentum. And momentum is a very good thing.

Never lose your momentum. I remember a time when I was moving along very well in business, and I was instructed by an "expert" to discontinue doing a certain business activity that was bringing me some degree of results and forsake it for a new modernized approach that would be more efficient and whatever. I followed their opinion, and I lost one of the most valuable things that a business person can have, and that is momentum. What I should have done is added to the already existing methods, added new methods to experiment with, perhaps expanding upon what's already known to work. But to go on blind faith in some expert's opinion proved to be devastating to my momentum.

Often this comes down to just being willing to go with your gut and to hold the course, to stick with what we know already works in our life. Yes, there are innovations, there are new things, but what I've come to find out is that quite often when people make hasty decisions that ultimately lead to compromising their momentum they make these hasty decisions out of *fear*. In fact, that's what I was approached with by this individual. There was some ulterior fear motivation that was going on behind the suggestion, which was not apparent to me.

And of course if you're a mover and shaker like me you like to be on the cutting edge. I have to be ever vigilant about watching my mind-thoughts and making sure that I'm not preoccupying myself with what somebody else is doing who is supposedly getting a result bigger or faster than mine, lest I fall into competitive thinking which immediately robs me of my self-confidence. Every time I have done that I have thrown away my self-confidence and I have slowed myself down, because we know that confidence, that feeling of certainty and expectation - that guaranteed future destination, is the magic potion that makes my work effective, that makes my actions the spontaneous right actions that I require to move myself forward.

Now perhaps other people have more business acumen or left-brained know-how than me in certain areas, and they can be very logical in their approach. They can be great assets as employees or contractors. My whole approach has been conceptual. It's based on what I feel confident in. When I feel certain and confident and expectant, I take actions that by some strange coincidence work out in my favor and move me in the direction of the goals that I say I want to reach. Never mind what the other guy is doing, and never mind the opinions or suggestions of other well-meaning people. Yes, have a look. Maybe incorporate something if it's congruent with our vision in addition to what we've already got. But haste makes waste, and in my case, haste made mega-waste - a wasteland out of my momentum, and a wasteland out of my productivity for a period of time. It led to me second-guessing myself. What a dreadful thing to do.

And then, because I tend to give my all to everything that I do, and because I was giving my all to a not so good suggestion, I began questioning my ability to even succeed. In fact, I had even forgotten what had originally worked! I had sold myself the lie that these old tried and true methods didn't work anymore and that everything has to be new and modern and we've got to figure stuff out because the world is changing so quickly. The bottom line is, I gave away my self-reliance and it cost me - I would estimate - millions of dollars. When you're on the move and reaching goals, don't even look sideways to see what other people are doing or the results that they are supposedly getting or what they think about your situation. When you're in momentum you maintain that momentum, period.

Another way to understand this would be: Don't compare your insides to other people's outsides. So many times people put on a good show. Look how great I am. Look how wonderful I'm doing. But deep inside, it's all a front. Deep inside they're wondering how *you're* doing so well and getting the results that you're getting. Again, this is the competitive mindset which cripples people. No long term business success can come out of this. This is a self-defeating mechanism. This is an equation that must lead to emotional deficit, not a good way to operate your life. Keep your own counsel.

Envy is ignorance; imitation is suicide.
Ralph Waldo Emerson (1803 – 1882)

I'm happy to announce that I've pulled my head out of my ass and remembered these tried and true methods that work and continue to work. I've reinitiated them in my business, and lo and behold, momentum. I thank God for my ability to think for myself. This is the main ability that has propelled me to reaching the heights of achievement that I have so far in my life. Yes, I *can* choose my course, I *can* make decisions and *I can hold myself to account.*

There are a lot of proponents of "life coaches" and people who are going to keep you on track or keep you motivated, or some kind of nonsense like this. You know, integrity is an inside thing. Again, it's not about giving away your responsibility to some outside phenomenon, some force outside of you, to do for you what you are somehow too weak to do for yourself. To be an inner-directed person means to be internally motivated - intrinsically motivated.

Now let me make this distinction: Breakthroughs in your thinking can come through other people. And all opportunities come through other people. So put yourself in that environment. Seek mentoring; seek people who are getting the result. (By their fruits you will know them.) But at no point would I suggest for someone to assume the posture that they cannot hold themselves to account. They just don't have a big enough vision for themselves if they need to be motivated by a coach. They just don't have a goal.

People often come to me looking for coaching, and many of them I turn down, because if someone is coming to me as a needy person, no matter what I do to "help" them, they are going to fulfill their self-image as a needy person. If they are *being* a needy person they are going to *do* what needy people do, and they are going to *have* neediness in their life. So I can't be in integrity and say, "Yes, I'll coach you and hold you to account for just doing the things that you know you could be doing all along."

Again, where is your answer? *You* are your answer. And how is it revealed? It's revealed by your action. Yes, my answer is revealed when I am in action. It's time for people to stop sidestepping their own power.

When I'm seeking wisdom in my life - when I go to great people for counsel or to bounce an idea off of a mentor - I do it as a result of being in action. It's not a passive thing. It's an active thing. It's a dynamic thing. I'm in action, I'm applying my best thinking, I'm getting these results, these ideas are coming up, and now I'm bouncing these ideas off of a person who's got an objective view and who is getting great results in their life.

These are often spontaneous mastermind sessions. In fact, the best masterminding that I've ever done has been spontaneous. It has not been a canned thing. There is no structure to it, and it's typically one-on-one or very small groups. When I'm at events (seminars, conventions, etc.) people often come up to me and want to have a conversation about something that's going on with them to get my feedback or ideas, or a reflection of themselves, or whatever they're looking for. Sometimes a large group of people gather around to hear the conversation, but typically it's just a few people (maybe poolside at a conference that I'm attending or speaking at) who find me, and we get to have an authentic conversation with no pretense or rank or labels. Simply an authentic conversation. These tend to be powerful experiences where people gain a whole new level of understanding on things. But at the same time, I can't give anything away. I learn lots from these interactions as well. And depending on the mental state of the person or people I'm speaking with, I could be making valuable observations of who they are, their self-image, and what kind of results they're getting.

For example, having been on the path for a while it becomes glaringly obvious to me when someone is using self-defeating language. A person's choice of language is very revealing if we're awake to it. So I choose to stay awake now. And because I'm awake to it I'm able to offer someone who may be asleep an opportunity to wake up through the observation of their language. One distinction could be a huge breakthrough. I know it's been that way for me. I'll take all the knowledge I can get *through my observation.*

People don't find opportunities for true mentoring, for true masterminding, by accident. They've put themselves in the environment for things like this to occur in their life. There's a saying, if you hang around the barbershop long enough you're going to get a haircut. If you play on the tracks, eventually there will be a train. So I'm a big proponent of seeking opportunities to be in the company of other high achieving people. I can identify these people by their results and by their language – again, by their fruits you will know them.

If I could go to a conference, seminar or workshop where people who are getting great results are going to be, where I could hear a great speaker or lecture that maybe gives me even one new distinction that could transform my experience of my relationships, perhaps one idea that could make me millions of dollars, what's that worth?

If you think education is expensive, try ignorance.
Benjamin Franklin (1706 – 1790)

So I am willing to pay the price of being the student. I'm constantly learning. I have not arrived. As soon as I'm manifesting fish and loaves I'll write a book about it, but right now, I'm very much on the path, willing to observe and willing to learn.

One other thing I feel I have to say about this idea - that there is a difference between "life coaches" and true mentoring – is that everyone has different strengths. I've said before that I'm good at a few things (in fact I'm tremendously good at a few things) and I'm completely disastrous at most (or ignorant at most). And is there anyone who can claim different? So, what are you going to get from a life coach? How to live? I believe in developing your strengths and managing your weaknesses.

So, various people in my life have a mentor role in various areas. There are people in my life who are my role models for generosity or intelligence or graciousness or patience or drive or confidence. I've got role models in these various areas of my life, and it's interesting, none of them have mixed into other areas. That doesn't mean that they're only good at one thing. That just means that the way they show up for me in my life, compared to where I'm at - from the position that I'm operating from - they are my ideal. They are my ideal in *that* one area, and other people are my ideal in *that other* area. None of them are my messiah. They are peers who I admire, and I model in those specific areas, and it has accelerated my growth tremendously.

You deserve to have people like that in your life, and become conscious of it. And before you know it, you're one of those people in the lives of others. You may already be. So let's acknowledge ourselves, and again, stop giving away our self-reliance, stop giving away our power, and stop giving away our responsibility because somehow we are not good enough. We are more powerful than we realize.

I'd like to conclude this chapter by going back to the original idea we opened it with. Can we have our passion, our fun, our abundance and our responsibility simultaneously? I have concluded by much observation that not only is the answer yes, but to deny ourselves in one area is to deny ourselves nonetheless throughout. The way to fulfillment is through the fulfillment of who we are. Compromising with this is futility. You are so capable!

-Simple Action-

Find an organization or a community of people who share similar values as you and get involved. This may be a business group, a humanitarian effort or whatever is congruent with where you're going in life.

Develop consistency and focus when performing the daily actions you have learned about throughout this book. Remember, consistency and intensity are the keys to progress.

FINAL WORDS

All I can say is thank you. Thank you for being someone who is willing to look, and willing to confront the urgent need for personal integrity in our society. As a person who chooses to take action on the ideas you have gained here and the vision that drives you, you have become a part of the solution on this planet. Once an individual develops their individual power, they are able to be powerful in their groups, in their nations and the human race as a whole. I applaud you. Now go out and make a difference in your life and the lives of others, and ultimately, others will applaud you too. Perhaps, in time, books like this will no longer be needed on this planet. In my lifetime? Who knows? My crystal ball is on back-order. So I'll keep charging ahead and welcoming those who also choose to do something with their life, reassuring them that they are not alone.

Namaste,

John Lavenia

For more information about John Lavenia's writings, courses, lectures and seminars please visit www.JohnLavenia.com.

RECOMMENDED READING

Think and Grow Rich, by Napoleon Hill

The Power of Your Subconscious Mind, by Dr. Joseph Murphy

The Seven Habits of Highly Effective People, by Stephen Covey

The Richest Man Who Ever Lived, by Steven Scott

Power vs. Force, by Dr. David Hawkins

Awakened Imagination, by Neville

Wake Up and Live, by Dorothea Brande

The Law of Attraction, by Michael Losier

The Seven Spiritual Laws of Success, by Deepak Chopra

The Problems of Work, by L. Ron Hubbard

Rhinoceros Success, by Scott Alexander

The Science of Getting Rich, by Wallace D. Wattles

You Were Born Rich, by Bob Proctor

The Traveler's Gift, by Andy Andrews

For an expanded list of recommended resources, including books and audio/visual products relating to specific categories such as business, spirituality and health, visit www.JohnLavenia.com.

Special Bonus for Readers of Integrity is Everything

* * * * * * * * * * * * * * * * *

As a thank you for purchasing *Integrity is Everything*, and as an opportunity to expand the usefulness of its contents in your own life, you are invited to participate in an exclusive weekly forum with author John Lavenia called *Iron Words*. In each session, John delivers ideas, discoveries and stories to raise your understanding and expand your application of success principles in daily life. This is available only through the website, and your enrollment is free!

www.JohnLavenia.com

In addition, John periodically offers courses, seminars and limited run products at a significant discount to his readers. These programs are made available on a first-come-first-served basis, and as a member of the *Iron Words* forum you'll be among the first to know.

Also included on the website is a collection of highly useful, time-saving tools for business builders worldwide. These include communication tools, marketing and lead-management tools, web development and much more. Just click on the *Free Resources* section.

* * * * * * * * * * * * * * * * *

Your access code for Special Offers is:

15961